My Child and Other Mistakes

My Child and Other Mistakes

ELLIE TAYLOR

HODDER*studio*

First published in Great Britain in 2021 by Hodder Studio
An imprint of Hodder & Stoughton
An Hachette UK company

1

A CIP catalogue record for this title is available from the British Library

Hardback ISBN 9781529362992
eBook ISBN 9781529363005

Typeset in Bembo MT Pro by Palimpsest Book Production Limited, Falkirk, Stirlingshire

Printed and bound in Great Britain by Clays Ltd, Elcograf S.p.A.

Hodder & Stoughton policy is to use papers that are natural,
renewable and recyclable products and made from wood grown in sustainable
forests. The logging and manufacturing processes are expected to conform
to the environmental regulations of the country of origin.

Hodder & Stoughton Ltd
Carmelite House
50 Victoria Embankment
London EC4Y 0DZ

www.hodder-studio.com

For VZ and PZ.

Contents

Introduction

Thanks for choosing to read my book or at least flick through it in a shop while you wait for it to stop raining.

In these chapters, you will find an incredibly unexceptional story told by an unqualified woman going out of her way to be extremely unhelpful. You're welcome.

It's the story of how an ordinary woman decided to become an ordinary mother to an ordinary baby. A story that takes place thousands of times every day in every country across the world. There she is, joining an unending line of matryoshka dolls splitting open to pop out another little figurine, who in turn pops out another little figurine, repeat ad infinitum until the Sun explodes/Earth explodes/we explode and our endless game of genetic copy and paste finally stops.

And therein lies the problem. This tale has been around for so long and been told so often that we are too jaded to see what it really involves. But scratch away at the layers of fluffy teddy bears and adorable teeny tiny sleepsuits, and eventually you'll reveal the tale hidden underneath: a brand new mother, freshly born herself, watching exhausted and astounded as the tectonic plates of her very existence shift beneath her. But that doesn't fit on a card from Funky Pigeon, does it.

So that is the story I am telling. It is both massive and

profound, and at the same time mediocre and humdrum. This book may not be useful in a 'Here's a Diagram on Perineal Massage' or '37 Steps to Safely Serve a Toddler a Grape' kind of way, but what it does do, I hope, is reflect back the quiet story of the exceptionally unexceptional experiences that so many mothers share.

As a cis white woman married to a cis white man who were fortunate to conceive naturally, my account of parenthood is undoubtedly limited by my many privileges. My hope, though, is no matter what your family looks like, whether you're a mum and a dad, or two mums, or a single parent involved in a passionate affair with Disney+, and regardless of whether you've had your child the old fashioned way or you've adopted, or you cooked up your sprogs with a surrogate, I hope that you can see a little of yourself in the story I describe. A story that, at its heart, is often universal. A story of how deciding to have a child can be a prolonged and agonising process rather than an enthusiastic swan dive into a world of soft play and pureeing. A story of how being a parent can mean the banal rubs up against the breathtaking twice before you've even had time to scoop the sleep out of your knackered, crusty eyes. A story of how you can think your kid is the best thing you've ever done while simultaneously thinking the little prick is the biggest mistake you've ever made. Because in many ways, my child, my darling Ratbag, really is a dreadful, dreadful mistake. And believe me, I have racked up some top-notch mistakes in my 27 years (plus another ten years).

My mistakes come in different forms. Some of them are so small and meaningless that I knowingly continue to repeat them, for example:

- Thinking I can make poached eggs
- Putting on red lipstick before brushing my teeth
- Trying olives
- Ordering jeans online
- Thinking it's OK to write 'lettuce know' instead of 'let us know' on formal work emails.

Then there are the mistakes that come in the form of one-offs that happened years ago but still have the ability to make me sweat with shame on random Monday mornings at 3.00 am, i.e.:

- The time I ran out of petrol in a traffic jam on a dual carriageway and, while attempting to get my phone from the back seat to call for help, managed to lock myself out the car. I then had to perch on my boot in my yellow anorak looking like a desexualised version of a 90s *Nuts* magazine photoshoot as confused drivers looked on at 1mph.

- The time at university when I insisted on cutting my friend's hair by making her stand in a bath and then slowly turn in a circle towards the snipping of my scissors. The resulting asymmetrical bob I gave her curly locks made her look like a cross between King Louis XIV and the sister with the 'pencil' hair-do in the penultimate episode of *Fleabag*. Needless to say, I am no longer in contact with either that girl or her hair.

- The time during a job interview for the role of a part-time library assistant, I was asked who inspired me, and my answer was the well-known literary trailblazer, Caprice.

– The time I bumped into an ex-boyfriend and, unsure how to end the awkward exchange, stretched out my arm to initiate a formal handshake (with a man I had lived with for two years and once shagged in the loos of the London Dungeon).

And then we come to the big mistakes. The *real* balls-ups. The mistakes I wish I could go back and undo but know that if I did, my life would be unrecognisable. Things like going to that particular university, studying that particular subject, saying yes to that job, saying no to that boy. These are complicated mistakes. They make me think, 'Perhaps I could have done things differently, but at the same time, I'm glad I made them because of where they led me. I'm glad I learned from them, and above all, I'm glad I have an anecdote about shagging in the London Dungeon.'

It's somewhere around here, in this complex and contradictory place of self-reflection, where I would file the decision to have a child.

In another life, there is the 'me' who opted to remain child-free. I daydream about that woman. There she is. Napping on the sofa, drooling gently onto an expensive velvet cushion she was able to buy because she doesn't have to worry about ever-present tiny hands covered in Frube. When that woman wakes, she'll leave the house, not accounting for her whereabouts to anyone. She'll amble to a café at her own pace by herself, not having to stop to look at each leaf on the ground that a small tyrant has pointed out, or create an origin story for a discarded McCoys packet that said small tyrant has spotted in a hedge. The woman will arrive at the café and choose what she wants to eat – not having to consider how long it may take to prepare and whether her constant miniature companion has the patience necessary to wait. The woman can sit on a high stool, not having to worry about a wiggly little person falling off. The woman can go to the loo by herself without a pint-sized narrator joining her in the cubicle, loudly asking why Mummy's front bot bot is spiky.

That woman has a perky rack, an unwearied face and shoes that are totally unsuitable for chasing after someone determined to capture a squirrel. The woman's bag contains an uncracked, fully charged phone and a novel she started a day ago that she's almost finished. The bag does not contain a small plastic tractor or a Tupperware of stale rice cakes, and neither does it hold a pack of wet wipes, a wizened conker, or a 'use in case of emergency' Kinder Surprise.

That woman's time is her own. All of it. That woman's headspace is her own. All of it. Her needs are the only needs she has to prioritise.

I look at that woman, leaving the café now, off back home to finish that book or order that expensive white cashmere jumper to go with her new dry-clean only white linen trousers, and I think two things.

1) What a lucky cow.
2) I'm glad I'm not her.

So, this is the story of how I made my most excellent mistake. A story of contradiction, of monotony, of wonder and of small people crapping on your carpet and then grinding it in with their foot like Sandy in *Grease* putting out a cigarette. A story I would have liked to have read when I was thinking about having a kid and one that would have offered me hope as a lost new mum. It's my spectacular boring story, but I really hope that sometimes, it's your spectacular boring story too.

I

Deciding

When my sister gave birth to her first child, I was 25 and working at a very serious TV news channel as a highly in-effective marketing assistant. My job involved lots of excellent transferable skills, like ordering mouse mats and Googling, 'What is marketing?' I can't remember what I was earning but I'd make a can of tomato soup last me two lunches, and would feel giddy with hedonism if I could afford a Babybel to drop in the middle.

When I got the call that my nephew had been born, I took the afternoon off work (the mouse mat backlog would have to wait) and on the way to catch the train to the hospital, I stopped at a fancy Soho bakery. I bought four delicious cupcakes, each one a different wildly exotic flavour. The lady serving me placed each cake carefully in a special box, sealed the box with a special sticker, and then put the special box with the special sticker inside a special bag. I spent more on those cupcakes than I would have spent on soup in a fortnight. And off I went to the hospital.

After I tracked down the maternity ward, I tentatively pulled open the curtains surrounding what I hoped was the right bed. Inside was quite the sight. Staring back at me was my box-fresh nephew in a Perspex cot, and beside him, my sister looking – and I cannot overstate this – like an absolute dog.

Physically, my sister Shona and I are very different creatures. I'm a massive wall of a woman: nearly six feet tall with industrial hips. My sister, on the other hand, is the runt of the litter. She's five feet six, 90% bone, 10% Parkrun. We like to put our physical differences down to the fact our mother smoked a little when she was pregnant with Shona. (It was the 70s. Be chill.)

It turns out my whippet of a sister had been cooking up a baby that was an absolute unit. This had led to a very rough birth that lasted around three lunar cycles and ended in a forceps delivery that ripped her so badly she was left with a 4th-degree tear that had to be repaired under general anaesthetic. All of that combined – the whopper of a baby, the sleep deprivation, the traumatic delivery – explained why the woman in the hospital bed staring back at me looked like Ronnie Wood in a maternity bra.

Gradually the hospital cubicle filled up. We were joined by my brother-in-law and my parents. There was laughing and crying and cooing and pooing. It was a momentous day for our family. The day my sister transformed from woman to mother. The day Mum and Dad gained a long-awaited promotion to grandparents. It was a distinct new period in the family story. A new paragraph starting with one of those enormous elaborately decorated uppercase letters you see in medieval documents, painstakingly illustrated in gold leaf by a blind hermit monk. A huge day. A massive day. A day of days. And yet, as I left the hospital and headed back home, the main thought circulating in my mind was not about my nephew or my sister, and neither was it about the majesty of new life or the quiet nobility of the female body. No. My one clear, overwhelming thought as I sat on the train home, was that no one had mentioned the cupcakes.

And that, I think, tells you everything you need to know about my interest in babies.

This might be a good point to mention that I am the youngest child and also the youngest grandchild on both sides of my family. A position I had always been more than content with. Sure, I was 25 and an extremely high-flying mouse mat executive, but I was still very happy bathing in all that glorious attention. I was the funny one. The silly one. The one who was a bit useless at everything but in a disarming way, thank you very much. And so, that day in the hospital, I was faced with an awful realisation. That from now on, anything and everything this newborn baby did would trump anything I could ever do. Even something amazing like buying four cupcakes.

A usurper had staged a bloody coup and in doing so had both ruined his mother's undercarriage and chucked me and my red velvet off our pedestal.

What. A. Knob.

As the weeks and months rolled by, my nephew resolutely refused to stop being younger than me. And so I gradually learnt to accept his snide existence. But that didn't mean I was enthusiastic about being an aunt. In hindsight, I cringe at what an arsehole I was to my sister in those early days and during her son's first few years.

As my nephew grew older, I remember having heated arguments with my sister where she'd tearily ask me why I wasn't like her friend's sisters who endlessly volunteered to babysit. Why didn't I want to make the trip back to Essex to spend time with my nephew and then, in turn, my new little niece? Didn't I love them? Didn't I care? To be honest, I didn't. I had grown to feel about them the same way I feel about anchovies – they aren't something I enjoy, and the smell of them can make me retch.

My detachment from her kids wasn't just about petty jealousy. It was also the fact that I had never hung out with a baby and had no desire to do so. I didn't know anything about babies, or how to interact with them, and I didn't have any desire to learn. I wasn't drawn to them like some of my female friends were, gagging to sniff a newborn's head like a coke addict snorting up gear midway through a bender.

For as long as I can remember, if someone showed me a picture of a baby, I felt nothing. However, if I'd been shown a picture of a cat, I could almost feel the fur growing on my ovaries. I'd want to kiss and cuddle all of the baby puddy tats. With baby humans, a curt head nod coupled with a 'How do you do?' was more my style. I had the maternal instinct of a pitta bread. I assumed it would change. I assumed that I'd hit 30, an alarm bell would sound, and I'd find myself hit with an overwhelming urge to start shooting out kids, my womb like a production line featured in *Inside the Factory*. I'd churn out baby after baby as Greg Wallace in a hairnet enthuses about the speed and precision of my labelling process. But it never happened.

I soon learnt that when I voiced this disinterest in having children, people often responded with discomfort. They would quickly dismiss what I'd said ('You don't mean that, you'll change your mind'), wanting to shoo the awkwardness away or, more often than not, laugh at the tales I'd tell about the awful things my evil nephew had gotten up to now. The innate attention-seeker in me enjoyed how much tension I could create with this subject, so I began to ramp up my act. Having my genuine uncertainty about whether or not I wanted kids disregarded by family, friends and co-workers – coupled with my hardwired need for the limelight – turned me into a caricature of a kid-hater. I became Essex's answer to Miss Hannigan, the gin-swilling, evil owner of the orphanage in *Annie*. The more I exaggerated my disgust of children, the more deviant I appeared, the louder the laughter. Great for stand-up. Less useful at lunch with your in-laws.

Women having the 'luxury' of opting out of motherhood is, in the grand scheme of human existence, an extremely recent development. To suggest you have no desire to procreate or that you've no natural yearning to fulfil the archetype of 'mother' can provoke a surprisingly strong reaction.

'What do you mean you don't want children? But you're a FEMALE WOMAN. With a WOMB. What else are you for? Please god tell us that you at least have a basic béchamel sauce recipe in your repertoire or you'll have to be exterminated.'

With new generations coming of age, the resolve not to have kids is undoubtedly a growing societal movement. Whether it's due to financial or environmental reasons or just being more mindful that parenthood doesn't have to be a certainty, more and more women are remaining child-free. One study found that the proportion of women who never have children has doubled in a generation. Hopefully this means that gradually the condescension and pity that my uncertainty was met with will ebb further away, leaving all women with room to question their attitudes towards repro-duction without fear of vilification, or unwanted and unnecessary sympathy. Children are not the only route to having a meaningful life as a woman. I had a meaningful life before I had a child, and had I not become a mother, my life would still have value, worth and love (and significantly fewer discarded raisins in my pocket).

I always batted my innate ambivalence towards kids being down to my nature, but I also think it's worth acknowledging that for a long time, my life simply wasn't set up for me to have a kid. I started dating my current husband, Phil, when I was 25, and he was 34. I was young and giddy with my lofty mouse mat ambitions, and he was a very clever, handsome journalist who had recently come out of a long-term relationship with a woman his age. In a classic man-in-his-30s move, he cleverly hitched his wagon to a younger female wagon with no immediate withering ovary concerns. Canny. There was zero reproduction desire from anyone here.

And we had a brilliant life. All we did was laugh and drink and then go on holiday to hot places where we'd laugh and drink – this time whilst wearing summer dresses (me) and sweating from the chest hair (me again).

Things were marvellous. I had begun to dabble in stand-up comedy and found, to my amazement, that there was a life away from mouse mats and bulk-ordering biros. Phil was supporting me in my new exciting career both emotionally (lovely) and financially (lovelier), and we were flying high. As relationships go, this one was a belter. In fact, things were going so well between us that, after two years, Phil moved to Moscow.

Oh.

He'd been offered a job he couldn't turn down, but we wanted to stay together. And that was that. For the next three years, we would stumble through a long-distance relationship, which I can highly recommend if you're into strange reunions where the love of your life with whom you've shared roll-on deodorant walks into your hotel room and feels as familiar as the maintenance man who's just been in to fix the air con.

I'd get so nervous at these occasional homecomings. I'd sit waiting for him in fancy London hotel rooms working out my plan of action. When he walks in, should I peck him on the cheek or flash him my boobs? I haven't seen him for two months. Maybe just one boob, then? That's right, isn't it? One tit for a boyfriend, half a tit for the air con man? Usually, I'd settle for something in the middle – a high five.

During those Russki years, I'd moved out of the apartment Phil and I had shared and moved into a flat-share with some of my best friends. I loved it. In an ideal world, I would still live in a commune of female friends today. I sometimes daydream about what it would be like. I imagine we'd hang out all day watching *This Morning*, French-plaiting our hair, discussing the importance of accepting the ageing process whilst simultaneously organising our next Botox bulk buy. Men would only be allowed in for very specific reasons i.e. smoochie-smoochie/explaining what AirDrop is.

My actual flat-share with my friends Julia and Sophie in Hampstead was almost as idyllic. We'd spend our weekends walking on the Heath, going for brunch and then coming home to make fancy recipes involving za'atar. As a trio, we became passionate about our niche viewing habits. We were obsessed with 80s BBC drama *Tenko*, that depicts a Japanese female prisoner of war camp during WW2. We'd discuss how truly awful it must have been to live through such a horrific experience, but on the other hand, marvel at how enviably thin the actresses playing starving prisoners were. Every cloud.

I was writing in the day and doing stand-up four or five

nights a week, slowly climbing my way up what comics call the LOL ladder (no one has ever called it that). Phil was living in a huge bachelor pad in Moscow and going on ex-pat nights out that would start at midnight. Hardly a mummy and daddy in the making. It's hard to underline how much kids weren't on either of our minds. We had zero interest and, crucially, zero space for a tiny person in our strange 'together but apart' relationship.

As time went on, with Phil and I still in different countries, I did start to get interested in getting engaged. Not an original desire for a 20-something woman, I'll admit, but it was always something I just assumed would happen. To me, it was inevitable. Everyone important in my life were married couples. My grandparents, my parents, Eamonn Holmes and Ruth Langsford. Kids, I wasn't sure about, but a ring on my finger to prove a man owned me? YES PLEASE. Sure, it's old fashioned and conformist but come on, you get a whole day where people legally have to tell you how beautiful you are while you act like a total cow to your bridesmaids when one of them misses a step in the routine you've choreographed to 'Boom Boom Boom' by The Outhere Brothers. Why wouldn't I want to do it?

I was aware, of course, that I could propose to Phil. After all, I'm a feminist and don't shave above the knee to prove it. I was an equal part of this equal relationship. I *could* have asked him. But I knew I never would. Because if I did, I would resent him for the rest of my life, which isn't the best way of entering into wedded bliss. I shamelessly and without embarrassment wanted a proposal. MY proposal. I'd gobbled up enough romcoms to know the 'correct' order of doing things. The grateful man proposes to the superior lady. It's basic physics.

And so, a mild itch began to form that only a proposal would scratch. When I examine why the itch flared up, I think it was threefold:

1) I was heading towards 30, an age when women famously explode into slime unless they are legally shackled to a man.
2) I was experiencing a simmering rage about clearly being incredible marriage material and, if Phil didn't want to hook this sexy fish, then he should, as Virginia Woolf once said, 'shit or get off the pot' (I am aware in this analogy that I am a toilet).
3) External pressure, both imagined and real.

Every day I would log on to Facebook (it was like the 17th century's equivalent of TikTok) and see another photo of someone I'd once met at a barbecue, waggling a fresh ring on a now very diamondy finger. Every day. Diamondy fingers up Welsh mountains. Diamondy fingers up Eiffel Towers. Diamondy fingers next to a carriage and a sad horse in Central Park. And always accompanied by a comment involving the bastardisation of some Beyoncé lyrics (that I refuse to recap here because you have to draw a line in the sand somewhere).

Every time I saw one of these pictures, my ancient un-engaged soul would take another swig from its bottle of Malibu while slurring the words to 'On My Own' from *Les Mis*. I remember a friend once sent me a screen grab of a Facebook status posted by a girl we'd gone to school with. She knew I'd hate-like it. She was right because it went a little bit like this:

'When we got to the beach, Rob pulled out ANOTHER engagement ring! Now I have two! Luckiest girl in the world! He must have really liked it, to have put TWO rings on it!'

As I read it, I vividly remember I was standing in my dressing gown in the kitchen eating a cold jacket potato like an apple. And at that moment, I discovered that I, too, had two things for this woman, and they were both of my middle (non-diamondy) fingers flicking her two big fat birds.

TWO RINGS. I couldn't even get *one* from my boyfriend and I'd hosted everyone's favourite TV makeover show with questionable feminist values, *Snog Marry Avoid*, FFS.

And that was just the randoms getting engaged. When the avalanche of nuptials began to collide with my closest friends, sweeping them up and spitting them out with a new prefix, well, that was even harder.

I was envious of them, happy for them and furious with them all at the same time. Envious of having a partner who had so willingly signed on the dotted line. Happy for their legally documented love. Furious when I saw how gleefully they severed their surname and hurriedly stitched on that of their new husband in its place.

The name changes really got to me. I didn't know these new women. Shelly Lloyd was the girl I went to school with. Who da fuq was Shelly Atkinson, and why was she sending me messages asking if 5.00 pm on Saturday was OK to drop round for a cuppa and had I tried the ratatouille recipe she'd sent me? 'GO AWAY WEIRDO,' I'd think. 'WHO ARE YOU?'.

I am territorial about my friends. My core group of mates are a noisy gaggle of Essex women I've been friends with since I was 11. Our friendship straddles the arc of our lives. From first periods and lengthy debates about the magnitude of picking Art GCSE over Drama, to eyebrow microblading disasters and end-of-days break-ups with absolute tools. We've watched from the sidelines as truly awful events engulf one of our pack, and swooped in en masse like a scene from a loo roll advert where a door opens and seven puppies come charging out at full pelt, full of love, enthusiasm and dribble.

There have been dreadful girls' holidays to Kavos, where we spent all our money on fishbowls of rancid cocktails called things like Handjob on the Beach, and ended up surviving on packets of Pasta 'n' Sauce made in the hotel room kettle. There have been brilliant girls' holidays to quaint towns in France, where our rooftop apartment provided a thrilling front row seat to an all-male threesome happening in the apartment opposite us. We came back with a few new tricks up our sleeves and an iron resolution to always close the curtains.

Through everything, they were and are my first loves.

My constants.

And one by one, as Phil and I trundled on 1500 miles apart, I saw these friends get engaged and then married. There they went, moving in and on with nice local boys who were keen to start nice, settled lives with their girls, whereas I'd picked a man from the other side of the world (literally – Australia) who had shown his love for me by moving alone to an authoritarian state.

After nearly five years together (three of those spent in different time zones) the mild 'itch' to get engaged was now more like the burning, stinging agony of a box jellyfish tentacle being dragged slowly over an eyeball.

Engagement was the subtext in every phone call. Even

when I would seem upbeat and light, cheerfully waving him goodbye on FaceTime by flapping a bingo wing (we all do Skype sex differently) I would be screaming inside, 'PROPOSE TO ME YOU BELLEND. I AM A RAY OF FUCKING SUNSHINE.'

It became a toxic subject. He would insist he was deeply committed to our relationship and assured me we'd marry in time, and I would say OK, waggle my arm fat, hang up and then cry mournfully to my housemates.

A few days before my 30th birthday, a friend – seeing that I was a bit blue about the whole situation – suggested that we go for drinks in Covent Garden. An evening of early celebrations and an opportunity to drunk-bitch about my shit of a boyfriend? I was in.

London's Covent Garden is famous for all sorts of street performers. If you're lucky, you'll see a woman in a ball gown belting out that song from the Honda advert whilst balancing on a tightrope and doing some fire-eating. It's a place of noise and bustle and drama. Which explains why, initially, I barely noticed the group of people start to surround the table my friend and I were sitting at, and begin to sing.

When I did clock them, I assumed they were some of the aforementioned street performers. But as the singing continued in quite a targeted fashion to only us, I decided that they were actually drama students doing something annoying. Any moment now, I thought, this little marketing stunt would end and a leaflet would be placed on our table with the details of their new show: a potted retelling of the novels of John le Carré through the medium of jazz and finger puppets.

Like any good Briton, I did the only thing I knew how to do in this awkwardly conspicuous situation: I stared fiercely into my friend's eyes and ignored them. But their singing kept getting louder. My attempts at conversation were now being held at the level usually reserved for a 2.00 am heart-to-heart in front of the DJ booth in Oceana. What was really weird was that my friend was now looking utterly petrified. She wasn't responding to anything I was saying. Why wasn't she ignoring them too? What was wrong with her? Had she forgotten how to be British? I knew she was half-Portuguese but surely she knew what was expected of her.

Now, when you see videos online of unsuspecting people caught up in the middle of surprise flash mobs, it looks like a joyous experience. 'All that seemingly spontaneous singing and dancing – how MAGICAL!' you think.

I'm a big flash mob fan. I wasted days of my life watching them online. Along with 'military reunions' and 'cats hiding in funny places', videos of flash mobs are my go-to pick-me-up.

'*Sure, my house has burnt down because my life savings hidden inside the bath panelling caught fire, but I've just watched a kid find her daddy hiding in her Wendy house when he was meant to be in Kabul, and now I'm looking at a long-haired tabby curled up in a colander and next up is a montage of a surprise choir welcoming people home in an airport arrival lounge. Best day EVER! . . . What? I've just been fired? Well, thank goodness I saved that clip of a litter of kittens being raised by a friendly sow!*'

But on that evening in Covent Garden, I discovered that if, like me, you find yourself in the middle of a flash mob *that you know nothing about*, your thoughts escalate quite quickly along these lines:

This is a bit weird. Why are they coming so close to me? God, they're loud . . . Why has my friend gone silent? . . . Oh shit. They're clearly from a satanic sect and have chosen us to be their next sacrifice. THE END IS NIGH AND I NEVER GOT THE CHANCE TO BE ON *PIERS MORGAN'S LIFE STORIES*.

The fear of my life ending in a demonic ritual of disembowelment abated when out of nowhere, my boyfriend tapped me on the shoulder, a huge smile on his face and said, 'This is all for you, Ellie', before popping the question.

Although, I think 'popping' seems too trivial a word to use for our situation. Bubble gum and weasels go 'pop'. Overdue proposals laced with resentment in stressful long-distance relationships do not 'pop'. I'll have another go . . .

. . . My boyfriend tapped me on the shoulder, a huge smile on his face and said, 'This is all for you, Ellie', before *detonating* the question.

Finally, dear reader, after five years together, he had proposed. And to be fair to him, he had done it in style because, well, he had to, really. Not only had he enlisted the help of my friend to ensure I was in the right place at the right time and organised the menacing flash mob, he had also arranged for the whole thing to be secretly filmed.

It's a very special thing to have captured on video forever. I love watching it back, seeing my husband's excitement, my phew-I'm-not-going-to-be-slaughtered happiness and the Italian family of tourists sitting next to us in the pub whose faces show complete disinterest throughout the whole thing, until just after I say, 'Yes! Yes, of course, I'll marry you!' when they start smiling – because the waiter arrives with their burgers.

My husband maintains arranging a flash mob is the nicest thing a man has ever done for me, which means he never has to do anything romantic ever again, and to his credit, he's really lived by that sentiment.

So that was that. We were engaged. We were delighted and excited and very soon, we were very drunk. We called my parents with the news ('About time') and then Phil's parents in Sydney ('Oh big bloody hell'). There was a ring on a finger and a date in the diary.

A year after that, Phil moved back from Russia, and we married a few days before Christmas. It was a gorgeous day tarnished only slightly by a rogue decision to have my hair styled far more formally than normal. When I reached the altar, a life-affirming moment I had imagined and longed for, the first thing I whispered into my dashing groom's ear was, 'I look like Margaret Thatcher'.

Finally, no more questions from friends and family about when he was going to propose. No more jokes from my dad that by the time Phil and I got hitched, we'd be old enough to have the honeymoon on a Saga cruise. I felt like I could catch my breath. I'd caught up to where I was supposed to be in life. I was married and living with my husband. I was like my friends. Both the external pressure and the pressure I'd put on myself was lifted.

I WAS FREE.

But not for long.

As the playground rhyme says, *'first comes love, then comes marriage, then comes Ellie with a little baby carriage'*. I don't know which baby carriage is being referred to here – perhaps a Bugaboo Bee, but regardless, a new pressure was forming.

After two years of marriage, I was 33, and by now, only two of my Essex friends were, like me, childfree. Like all marginalised groups in society, we set up a WhatsApp support group. It was called 'The Patsys' after our hero, Patsy from *Absolutely*

Fabulous. The profile picture was a photo of her asleep in a skip.

The group began as a way to chat about things away from our knackered parent friends who were in the midst of sleep regressions and leaking. We swapped messages about boozy nights, lie-ins and how we never felt like we were going to piss ourselves when doing a jumping jack.

But as time went on, and we found ourselves undeniably heading towards our mid-30s, The Patsys chat began to change. It morphed into a space where we'd send obscure articles we'd read online at 3.00 am about how apparently easy-peasy it was to get pregnant after 35 and how Celine Dion had twins when she was 42 and how we still had ABSOLUTELY DEFINITELY LOADS OF TIME TO HAVE A BABY.

Both mine and Phil's families also seemed to be panicking on our behalf too. And they weren't subtle about it. They'd all seen how long it took us to get married, and this fuelled them to go on the attack with the delicacy of a slut drop. A prime example of this was my mother spending her and my dad's 40th wedding anniversary telling Phil, (and I am quoting verbatim here, so if you wince at the wording, please send your letter of complaint to ElliesMum@askjeeves.net) that he needed to hurry up and get on with 'spreading his sperm'.

If you need to take a minute to dry heave into a hedge, please go ahead.

What a verb choice. 'Spreading'. She made it sound like jam. It also suggests a bit of haphazardness, like Phil should be dolloping it out all over the shop as though it didn't matter if I was the vessel who had the baby. At this point, any baby that had been created by Phil's Bonne Maman raspberry conserve was better than nothing.

My sister was just as bad. For years she had been saying to me, 'By the time you have a baby, your nephew will be at university'. I always wanted to say back, 'Hmm, will he though? Because I've read his homework . . .'

On Phil's side, my mother-in-law had been after grandchildren since around the time he'd grown his first pubic hair. To be fair to her, she'd never hidden her hopes from us, and they really spilled out one Christmas morning. Sitting round the Christmas tree at their home in Sydney, a glass of Buck's Fizz in hand, I opened a present from his mum addressed to both Phil and me.

Inside the wrapping paper, I found a copy of the book *Secrets of the Baby Whisperer*.

Just to reiterate – at this point Phil was still in Russia and me in the UK. There was no baby and absolutely zero plans for a baby. At this juncture, my womb was like a London penthouse owned by an off-shore business magnate: vacant for the foreseeable future.

Staring at a newborn sleeping peacefully on the cover of the book, I had no idea how I was meant to react. The Buck's Fizz wasn't helping, so I found myself mentally zipping through a Rolodex of behaviours I could respond with; I could do some basic-bitch 'HAHA YOU ARE SO FUNNY' gratitude or perhaps a bit of Hugh Grant confusion or a lovely bit of textbook mother-in-law-backlash along the lines of: 'Well, seeing as we're giving people things they don't need right now but might do in the future, here's a pamphlet about choosing the right care home'.

Turns out I didn't need to reply with anything because when Phil saw the book, he spat out his outrage.

'Mum! Why did you get us this?!'

To which she cheerfully replied, 'Well, sometimes accidents happen.' Accidents happen. Her genuine response. Nothing like a traditional Christmas Day wish for an unplanned pregnancy.

I thought it was bad back then. But once we were married, the parents-in-law's desire for a new heir ramped up to DEFCON 1. We would FaceTime them every couple of weeks, and each call would feature a heavily awkward moment where one of them would say, 'So . . . any news?' And every time we'd have to tell them that, no, there was no news unless they wanted to hear about the council's proposal to switch our black bin collections from once a week to fortnightly. They did not want to hear about the bins.

Plus, all my friends just kept on doing it. Child after child. Before long, even one of the Patsys went over to the dark side. I haven't experienced that level of peer pressure since I got a henna tattoo on my lower back during that Kavos holiday in 2002.

And all the while, Phil and I were trying to work out what having kids would mean for us. How on Earth would we make it work? How could they fit into our lives? We both travelled so much – his work hours completely dictated by the news agenda and mine often taking place during the evenings with no routine whatsoever. How could a kid ever slot into our weird, messy lives? And more importantly, did we even want a child?

Tellingly though, something within me had started to shift because now when I saw a baby in a café, while my ovaries remained very much, 'new phone, who dis?', my brain was interested. I began to stare at kids in the same way I would stare at a piece of flat-pack furniture before assembling it.

Trying to work out if I had the patience and correct Allen key to make this chest of drawers. Assessing that if I did, would it be worth all the effort in the first place? What if I put it together really badly? What if I hated it when it was made? What if the drawers ruined my career or put too much pressure on my marriage, or what if it got ill or wanted facial piercings or didn't like musical theatre?

And then I got a message. On the Patsy WhatsApp group. By this point, it wasn't really a group anymore because there were only two of us left, and you can't have a group of two. That's why Howard isn't legally allowed to leave Take That. The remaining Patsy said that she didn't know how else to tell me, so here goes – she was going to have to leave the group because she was pregnant. With twins. What an exit.

I began to up my recon. Night vision goggles and full camo. Gradually, and in keeping with my painfully negative and controlling nature, I began to consume everything I could on birth and beyond. I still wasn't interested in the actual babies bit of having a baby (pure detail), but I was consumed with investigating the background, the experience, the practicalities.

The trouble with research is sometimes you can get bogged down in it. Too many facts and considerations can paralyse you. I was immersing myself in articles that estimated the average cost of raising a child until they're 18, to be around £70–£80,000. I then read another article saying that actually £70–£80,000 is the estimate for boys only, and that girls, in fact, cost parents around £108,000. Jesus Christ. I knew I'd gotten through my fair share of Rimmel Heather Shimmer Lip Gloss in my teenage years, but this gendered difference seemed extraordinary. Then I started reading up on the birth process and discovered that 90% of women tear during childbirth, with

20% of mothers still experiencing urinary incontinence ten years after their child was born, and an unlucky 3% having faecal incontinence as a glorious reminder of their child's original birthday. Then I looked into the effect that having kids has on relationships, reading that around two-thirds of married couples said the quality of their relationship nose-dived before their child turned three.

As a woman who very much enjoyed a great relationship with her husband, intact toileting abilities and the occasional frivolous shopping spree in Zara Home, my research was compelling in all the wrongs ways.

In the end, the thing that pushed me over the edge when deciding if I should try to get pregnant was a conversation I had with my mother. We were sitting in my tiny garden in Hackney, she was talking about me having kids (as bloody always), and I was saying I couldn't feasibly see how we could manage a baby around our jobs. I was going round and round in circles about how exorbitant nursery costs were, and how their opening hours probably wouldn't work for both mine and Phil's complicated work schedules, when my mum gently stopped me. She said that if I waited for the perfect answer to how it would all work, quite simply, I would never have a child. I said that my concerns weren't just logistical, and I was just about to whip out my new-found fun facts on faecal incontinence when she stopped me again. She told me not to think about this decision in terms of what my life would look like imminently if I decided to have a child but what it would mean for my life when I was her age. How did I want my life to look in the future?

I thought on that a lot. I understood what she meant. I'd done all the groundwork. I knew everything I needed to learn. Much like when Phil knew he had to propose or face the loss of this hot piece of Brentwood ass – in terms of having a baby, I knew the time had come for me to shit or get off this particular pot.

I decided that, while I wasn't 100% sure and still wasn't innately drawn to children, I knew that when I imagined myself at my mum's age, I was surrounded by a family I had made. I knew (and prepare for a nice bleak image here) that I couldn't imagine dying having not been a mother. Told you. Bleak. But unarguably a decision (of sorts). Phil, on his own route of pondering, had begrudgingly come to the same conclusion.

And so that was that. Here we were at last, sitting on the metaphorical pot together. We joined metaphorical hands, and the metaphorical straining began.

2

Trying

Once we decided to try and get pregnant, in a signature Ellie move that I like to call 'Armageddon Approacheth', I became obsessed with the idea that I wouldn't be able to get pregnant. Always on brand.

On my bad days, I'd think, 'I'm 34 – why didn't I do this a decade ago?? That would have been a much better idea! When I was young and ripe and earning 80p a month, and living with a boyfriend who used to come home from strip clubs smelling of tequila and infidelity – that would have been a much better time to start a family! God, I'm such an IDIOT!'

I began to panic about my eggs. What if I didn't have any left? What if I'd left it too long and they were on the turn? A bit like bacon when it develops that green sheen on it. You wouldn't risk it in a carbonara, would you?

It's impossible to reach adulthood these days without absorbing and internalising the general fear-mongering that laces discussions about women having kids past 30. Over the years, I'd read so many feature pieces and heard so many things on TV involving the general 'fact', that once a woman hits 30, her fertility drops off a cliff like a sleepy lemming. But if you delve a little deeper, the statistics seem cheerier. One study the NHS points to, states that for couples aged 35–39 who are having regular unprotected sex, 82% of them will conceive after one year, and 90% within two years.

Not too shabby at all for 35-and-overs (a new X *Factor* category). It suggests how fertility decline in women is more gradual than the pervading scaremongering would have us believe – it's not like the McDonald's Breakfast Menu: the clock strikes 11.00 am, and your chance of an Egg & Cheese McMuffin is over for EVER.

Judgement and pressure around having kids, however, seems pervasive at every part of a woman's fertile life. Have kids when you're deemed too young and be warned that your career is over before it's begun; you haven't experienced your own life, so how can you create a new one? Wait a little longer, and then worry that if you do get pregnant, you risk your career stalling compared to your male contemporaries? Or do you wait a few *more* years until you've properly established yourself, only to be told you're leaving it too late, that you'll be a knackered old parent who won't be able to run around with your child and play football (it's always bloody football) and risk having no option but IVF?

IVF can be an arduous, emotional and draining experience for couples, and with inconsistencies across the UK about who is eligible for it on the NHS, and how many rounds they are entitled to, it can be stressful in a multitude of ways. However, what an option to have. I have three friends who experienced fertility issues and ended up with very wanted NHS IVF babies.

But what happens if you are a single woman and want a child? Or an older woman in a relationship with someone you aren't 100% about – is a child with someone-but-not-The-One better than no child at all? Far too often, the responsibility for and the focus of 'fertility' as a subject seems to be lobbed at women for them alone to deal with. I think it's safe to say that not many men are lying about their age on dating apps in order to avoid repelling potential suitors with the chiming of their biological clock. Few men know what it's like to experience a barrage of targeted pregnancy test pop-up adverts to helpfully remind them that even the marketing world thinks they need to hurry the fuck up. Single men don't need to consider the murky world of egg freezing, which seems to walk a tricky line between offering a genuine option to child-free single women while at the same time monetising their fears.

In the UK, since 2012, the number of women having their eggs extracted and stored in deep freeze for potential future use, has more than doubled. But while more women are undertaking the process and 'egg freezing' becomes a phrase many would now be familiar with, even within the world of fertility science, there are debates over how successful egg freezing is. If the experts can't agree, then what chance do the women looking into egg freezing have of truly under-standing what they are buying into? How is 38-year-old Joanne Bloggs from Luton supposed to determine which clinic and doctor to trust? Joanne, who works in HR and whose entire medical knowledge consists of eight seasons of *Grey's Anatomy* along with witnessing someone perform the Heimlich manoeuvre in a Wimpy in 1997. Joanne, who isn't sure if she even wants children but keeps seeing her Instagram feed invaded by 'fertility checker' adverts when all she wants to do is look at photos of her friend's new kitchen island while eating a Twix in her pants. The really crap thing is, whether Joanne fully understands the science or not, what other options do single women like her have? If Joanne isn't certain she wants a child, she can either do nothing and see what happens *or* she can freeze her eggs, therefore hedging her bets and giving her some say over the shitty, pressured hand that biology has dealt her.

In the US, of those women who've had their eggs frozen, it's estimated fewer than 15% have actually used them, suggesting that for many, the process remains more hedge betting than family planning. I wonder if, for some women, the sense of control and definitive action that freezing offers is as important as the eggs themselves. Whether the eggs make it out of the deep freeze is one thing, but at least those women who want children will know that they did as much as they could. I am, of course, not saying that single women who don't freeze their eggs aren't 'trying' hard enough. I can think of many different reasons why a woman wouldn't want to undergo the procedure, including, 'Why bloody should I?', 'The science is unclear', 'I want things to happen naturally' and, the trickier, 'I don't have the money'. With egg freezing not available on the NHS (aside from some medical exceptions) and the cost averaging over three grand, it is a privileged option available to the few. From so many angles, fertility is an unfair and unbalanced dilemma often left for women to shoulder emotionally and, it seems, financially.

I was aware that if I were to get pregnant, I was heading towards the glorious land I'd heard referred to as 'geriatric pregnancy' – the label used for pregnancy in women over 35. Thankfully, the term is now deemed outdated, and its use is largely relegated to Katherine Heigl movies from the early 2000s. Older pregnant women are instead now referred to as having 'advanced maternal age', which I think, if anything, is worse – and definitely more dull. At least 'geriatric' provides some pantomime gasp value.

It wasn't, however, just my own decrepit fertility I was concerned about, as, by this time, my husband was 43. On my positive days, my brain would say: 'Chillax E-Dawg, you know men can have kids until they're ancient – look at Mick Jagger, he had a baby a couple of years ago, and he looks like he's been dug up from a grave. Phil will be sweet.' But on my blue days, I had concerns that his wrigglers may just be a bit past it. In keeping with the theory that from a medical point of view, fertility is largely treated as a woman's issue, the effect of age on male fertility is far less clear than the stats on the effect of age on female fertility. Nonetheless, I began to imagine his sperm doddering around. There they were – one had reading glasses, one had recently undergone a hip replacement, and the remaining one was researching camper-vans and yelling about immigration.

One in seven couples in the UK sadly experience fertility problems, with a quarter of these, never getting an explanation for their issues conceiving, so if we were to require any extra help, we figured time was of the essence to start trying.

We formulated a plan. We had a month-long trip to Sydney booked, so we decided to treat that trip like a final hurrah. In those last four last weeks of Aussie freedom, I would drink all the booze, scoff kilos of rare meat and carry as many heavy suitcases as my heart desired before coming back and getting very serious and, hopefully, very pregnant. But in the mean-time, I would do some groundwork in preparation. Step one was to 'Get to know "My Cycle".'

How did I get to know it, you ask? Well, the old-fashioned way, of course. I took My Cycle out for a drink where we spoke about our hopes and dreams. We had long heart-to-hearts in deserted car parks late at night where My Cycle sang for me and told me about its ambitions to become a star. I told My Cycle it had a beautiful nose, and it laughed coyly, saying no one had ever said that before. Oh, hang on, I think I'm mixing up My Cycle with the plot of *A Star is Born*. Let's try again.

How did I get to know My Cycle, you ask? Well, in the only way I know – an unnecessary amount of research, throwing money at the problem and, most importantly, some urine. Every day I would wee on a stick and shove it in a very expensive fertility tracking monitor where messages would flash up on a screen informing me if I was having a low fertility day, a high fertility day, or, best of all, a PEAK day.

I did that for a couple of months and, for the first time in my life, began to appreciate how narrow the window of time is for getting knocked up. For me, it seemed to be about three days per cycle. That's it. THREE DAYS. My two main thoughts were:

1) How have humans managed to procreate so rapidly when each month our eggs have a shorter shelf life than a profiterole?
2) If teenage Ellie had known this, she could have really chilled out on her morning-after pill consumption.

Teenage me was utterly petrified of getting pregnant. It was a constant and very real fear. Every month, I would await my period with a visceral feeling of dread. I often seemed to be due on a Saturday when I would be doing my weekend shift at my local Boots Pharmacy branch. I worked largely on the photo counter (which seems like an archaic job now, like chimney sweeping or working at Blockbuster).

I'd fritter the morning away in the shop usually by opening a camera too early and subsequently wiping a week's worth of someone's holiday snaps from a Canary Island. If I was lucky, I'd get demoted to a quiet stint refilling the incontinence pads, which usually ended with me hiding in the stock room scoffing some stolen Shapers strawberry nougat bars.

My aim on these Saturday mornings was to burn time until my coffee break when I'd be able to race to the loos, whip down my knickers and study the gusset with the focus of a forensics officer searching a patch of woodland for a blunt instrument. My heart would thump heavily as I hunted for some sign, ANY sign of blood. The tiniest display of anything that looked vaguely pink would cause a toilet cubicle cele-bration – like a silent version of a footballer sprinting towards their home fans, pointing their fingers to the sky and yelling, 'GET IN! I'M BLEEDING YOU BEAUTIFUL BASTARDS! COME ON YOU REDS!'

If, however, the gusset inspection (Gusspection™ E. Taylor) revealed nothing, and the follow-up loo roll wipe left the paper whiter than a 90s panel show lineup, then my heart would sink. I'd trudge back to the shop floor with a stomach full of anguish and another stolen Shapers bar.

Going back on shift, I'd stand at the photo counter on autopilot, asking people if they had an Advantage Card, while on the inside screaming, 'SHITTTTTT'. Clearly, I was incred-ibly pregnant, and my life was ruined. I would now never achieve all my great 17-year-old dreams, like going to univer-sity, creating real change in the world and/or becoming an FHM High Street Honey.

After a couple of hours providing some mournful photo-graphic advice, it would be my lunch break and back to the loos I'd dash, to go through the exact same process as earlier. Inevitably, the Gusspection (let's get it trending) would reveal the longed-for tiny red blob. After punching the air and promising the universe/Jesus/my idol Geri Halliwell that I would spend the remainder of my life atoning for this great mercy, I would spend the rest of the day beaming like I was a semi-finalist in the Miss Congeniality Pharmacy Setting Competition, Mid Essex Division, 2001.

(Years after, while telling a girlfriend about these anxious Saturday stints, she asked, as I worked in an actual chemists, why I hadn't used my thieving skills to pilfer a pregnancy test as opposed to low-calorie snack bars? I replied it probably had something to do with not being able to eat a pregnancy test.)

I cannot overstate how, for a few years of my life, getting pregnant was genuinely my biggest fear, just ahead of 'shark attack' and 'wasp caught up floaty dress'.

Gradually, though, my fear abated, when I realised that I was gifted at one particular thing. We all have individual skills. Some people are great at parallel parking; some people can say 'chorizo' in a Spanish accent without sounding like a twat; *my* god-given skill is that I am exceptionally good at taking the contraceptive pill. So good, that I used to think I deserved a reward for always remembering to take it. (Arguably, there was a reward, and it was the years I spent not having to watch *Mr Tumble* or sponge a tiny person's poo off my dressing gown.)

I still don't quite understand women who are on the pill but forget to take it. Don't get me wrong, I forget things. My keys, my wallet, the fact I'm married, sure. But forgetting to take something that could prevent you from *creating a human* who could one day look at you, then turn to a doctor and say, 'Turn the machines off – it's what she would want.'? I'm going to remember that.

Obviously, though, it does happen.

A woman I used to work with during my mouse mat years got pregnant after forgetting to take her pill. I remember chatting to her in the office kitchen as she rubbed her bump and laughed, saying how she just had a really bad memory. I felt like saying, 'Well that's funny, Jenny, 'cos every day you manage to remember to steal my milk, don't you? Maybe if you Sellotaped your packet of Microgynon to my semi-skimmed, Stephen in IT wouldn't be telling everyone how you've trapped him.'

While I am an excellent pill scoffer and appreciate the liberation that the medication gives to women, the fact that decision-making around contraception so often falls to women continues to get my goat. Just another thing to be filed under the title, 'FAO the Bitches'. While we are obviously fortunate to live in an advanced scientific era, so many contraceptive options open to women are, in one way or another, invasive. Whether it's ingesting synthetic hormones on a daily basis, having a strange *Black Mirror* implant in your arm, or getting a coil fitted inside your womb, they all require some form of sacrifice. Even writing the words, 'getting a coil fitted', makes me physically cringe – it sounds so mechanical – like something that should be happening to a transit van, not a uterus.

Of course, there are many men who take the lead and are excellent condom-wearers or brilliant puller-outers, but those options don't require intrusive procedures or prolonged digestion of chemicals that must be taken every day, with zero acknowledgement or gratitude from their partner. If I had my way, in any male/female relationship where the woman has taken up the mantle of contraception, there would be a formal ceremony every month where the man stands up in front of her (yes, I watch *Love Island*), thanks his love for both her sacrifice and service to their sex life, presents her with flowers and a box of Lindor Balls and then leaves her alone for the evening to watch something featuring Tom Hardy. (Exceptions will be granted for males willing to have a vasectomy – any man so hungry to bonk bareback that they'd let a medical professional make incisions into their scrotum deserves some Lindor Balls of their own).

By the time I was ready to actively try to make a baby at 34, I had been on the pill for about seventeen years. Seventeen years of militant anti-babymaking, that had to now be turned on its head overnight.

It reminded me of the highly festive family movie *Home Alone*, where Kevin McCallister (the tiny hero played by Macaulay Culkin) starts out incredibly scared of the creepy old man who lives next door. However, by the end of the film, we come to learn that the creepy old man is actually a misunderstood chap with a heart of bloody gold and someone who Kevin now thinks of with huge affection. That is very much the journey I went on with sperm.

Years of, 'CHRIST, GET IT AWAY FROM ME!', to, 'COME ON IN, IT'S LOVELY AND UNHOSTILE IN HERE!' Suddenly sex had gained a real purpose. A reason. Don't get me wrong, I've had sex for other reasons before, but they were fun kinds of reasons like because I was drunk, or for revenge. This was THE reason. The main 'fulfilling my ultimate purpose as a humanoid' reason.

I told my husband that there was no fun to be had during this serious intercourse. Imagine talking dirty while trying to conceive – that's bad parenting before you've even become a parent.

In my head, I built up making-a-baby sex as something extremely solemn. Something to be done in the dark, in silence, with your eyes closed. Three or four thrusts max, followed by the man declaring: '. . . It is done.' There would then follow an end of match handshake before both retiring to separate rooms and lighting candles in memory of your disposable income.

Needless to say, I was overthinking it all. But the first attempt was approaching and, lo and behold – right on cue – I weed on a stick and the dictator-fertility-machine-thing blinked back at me with the word: 'PEAK'. Ready the engines.

As it turned out, making-a-baby sex was exactly the same as normal sex, just with more existential angst, a headstand at the end and my husband whispering the words, 'Swim my little champions'.

But this turned out to be a practice round. A couple of weeks later, my period came.

How weird to see the usual red and, for the first time, greet it with disappointment and not relief. Not that I felt any real sadness, just a sort of, 'Oh. Right'. Like when your pizza arrives in a restaurant, and you realise you've ordered one with a white base.

Oh. Right.

Better luck next time.

The next time, however, was a little trickier because I was travelling around the UK on a tour of my stand-up show, which was, ironically, all about whether or not I wanted to have children. Never trust a comic. Dirty liars the bunch of us. By my calculations, looking at my gig list and tracking My Cycle, if I was lucky, I'd be ovulating during a cluster of tour dates that were close enough for me to travel home from each night. This, of course, meant easy access to my husband and, more importantly, his semen.

One of the tour dates that particularly sticks in my mind was in Aylesbury, Buckinghamshire (the town is recognised as the spiritual cradle of the Paralympic Games and famous residents include Brendan Cole and David Jason, don't you know). On the morning of the Aylesbury gig, I woke up with a sharp pain in the right-hand side of my abdomen.

As the day wore on, the pain was bad enough for me to call both my agent and my tour promoter to warn them that I thought I might have appendicitis and was considering going to A&E. We all agreed to see how it went for the rest of the day and make a call closer to kick off. When the time came for me to either jump on the train or call off the gig, I decided to plough ahead, assuming that even in a worst-case scenario Buckinghamshire must have some sort of rudimentary health care system, even if it was just an elder of the village (Brendon Cole) to act as a shaman.

The gig was fine, my appendix didn't explode, and I was home just after midnight to be reunited with my husband's penis, which was wearily waiting up for me.

Fast forward to a couple of weeks later, and I'm in the bathroom about to have a shower. That evening, I'm due to guest on a podcast that is recording in front of a live audience in a bar.

After our trip to Australia, where I'd drunk like a footballer with the keys to a Tiger Tiger, I'd drunk no alcohol except my conciliatory pizza-with-a-white-base G&T the month before. Standing in the bathroom, I start to think how lovely a big fat vodka and Diet Coke would be that night in the pub. I'm clearly not preggo, I think. I don't feel different at all and haven't been visited by any archangels, so a delicious voddy is very much ahoy.

But just to be sure, I think, I'll do a pregnancy test. My magic machine does those too. So, like I've been doing for the last few months, I widdle away and then shove the stick into the slot. A beep. A pause. Then . . .

PREGNANT.

That's all the screen says.

A big fat white cross on a purple background and the words PREGNANT in the middle.

Holy mother of Lorraine Kelly. A million things race through my mind, ranging from, 'Flipping bloody crap bags', to, 'Sigh, I really fancied a vodka,' but mostly, 'We've only tried for two months – Christ, we've gotten lucky'. I was very aware that some women wait years to see that much wanted positive test, and I felt incredibly blessed that due to sheer good fortune I'd gotten here so quickly.

Phil has left for work. He's been reporting on the Russian Novichok nerve agent poisonings and is on his way down to Salisbury to continue his coverage. We are in the middle of text chat. Just to underline how much I hadn't expected to see a positive result – while I was waiting for the machine to do its thing, I'd been sending him photos I'd taken the night before of him eating custard directly out of the pot and covering his face like a shamed celeb. How do you tell the person you are at your silliest with the most grown-up news you can imagine?

I snap a photo of the machine's screen with the word PREGNANT. I am about to send it to him. But then think, no. I can't go from custard to pregnancy. That's an awful segue. I must be thoughtful about the way he receives this life-altering news. So I message him:

'Can you talk? We have a situation.'

He replies immediately with:

'Not really, on the train.'

I obviously interpret this as, 'Yes, now is a perfect time to call.' So I sit on the stairs wrapped in a towel and tell the father of my child that he is going to be the father of a child.

First, there's silence. And then there is laughter.

There he is. Sitting in the quiet carriage. On the way to report on an attempted murder by foreign operatives. And laughing and laughing and laughing. He says it's wonderful news, and I say his champions really did swim, and he says of course they did, they're Australian and had I never heard of Ian Thorpe? And I say no, but later Google Ian Thorpe and belatedly think that it was a solid joke.

We giggle some more and swear a lot, and then he says, 'Well, that's that then. The dice is rolled,' which is a perfect way to end this scene.

Fade to black.

Now call me an old witch (OLD WITCH), but I think the pains I had on that Aylesbury shag day were actually ovulation pains. I've never had them before. I've never had them since. I like to think that it was my body trying to grab my attention.

'This egg, Ellie,' it was saying, 'it's this painful little egg that will make you a mother . . . hang on . . . why is she getting her phone out . . . why is she on NetDoctor . . . what's she searching for? . . . Appendic— NOOOO!! Oh, for god's sake! This is what I have to work with.'

The day zipped by filled with lots of filmic smiling at myself in the mirror and looking on Etsy for crocheted baby hats in the shape of Yoda ears. That night, I went to the podcast recording in the bar, ordered a soda and lime, and spent the whole thing screaming in my head: 'I'M MOTHER FLIPPING PREGNANT, YOU KNOBHEADS!'

The gig happened. I had fun, but was definitely slightly removed from the situation, too busy thinking of a thousand questions that would never be answered in a Be at One in Soho.

Would the baby make it? What would I look like with a bump? Will I start puking soon? Why haven't I been puking? What would we call it? When can I tell my mum? Will it love me? What will it look like? Will it be happy? Will it provide me with Instagram content?

I caught the train home and waited on the sofa for Phil to get back from Salisbury. My brain was too active for TV so I picked up my phone and Googled what a foetus the age of mine would look like. What I found were images that looked like an insect crossed with a baked bean. I made a mental note not to look that up again and quickly closed my phone.

It all felt surreal, just sitting there. Nothing and everything had changed.

There was only one thing for it. Food.

I went into the kitchen, poured myself some cereal and sat at the counter, just as I had done 12 hours earlier when I'd sat here at breakfast. Except this morning, I was one person. And now I was two.

I heaped on some sugar. It was the least I deserved.

No. It was the least *we* deserved.

3

Telling

Once my husband arrived home on the evening of the pregnancy reveal, we had a big cuddle and then a big heart to heart. We shared our excitement and worries, and Phil asked for some time to get his head around the whole idea.

It was at this point I discovered that even though I was the majestic vessel of new life, I may actually have to consider how my partner felt towards MY pregnancy. This wasn't something I had previously contemplated. Eugh. As we lay in bed that night, we knew that I was only about two or three weeks pregnant. Phil asked if the delicate news of this intensely private matter could remain just between us for the moment. I held his hand and said, 'Of course. It'll be our secret,' knowing that I'd already sent two friends a 'Guess what? I'm knocked up!' text.

In my defence *puts hands on hips in power stance*, I only told them because . . . well, because I wanted to. Plus, one is based in Kuala Lumpur, so doesn't count because she lives nine hours in the future, and the other is useful because she's a doctor and offers a bespoke NHS VIP service that, on one occasion, involved me showing her a photo of my perineum in Wagamamas. Both were also pregnant. Strategic, you see. But even after telling those two wonderful women, who said all the right things ('Amazing! You'll be brilliant! Yes, we miss vodka too!') and sent all the correct emojis (heart, smug pregnant lady, whale) and despite Phil's protestations, I still felt full to burst with the news of the life inside me. I wanted to tell everyone, and Phil wanted to tell no one. It demonstrates how so often we come at things from completely different approaches. For example:

He is considered and private.

I am rash and open.

He processes thoughts internally.

I process thoughts via Instagram stories.

He is measured and discreet.

I show my friends photos of my perineum in Wagamamas.

I tried to keep my feelings tempered. 'Hopefully optimistic' was the phrase Phil would use.

Just to give a little trigger warning here – I'm going to talk about the sadness of baby loss, so if you'd rather not read, please do skip the next few pages. I'd had a few friends who'd sadly lost babies in pregnancy, and I was all too aware of the fragility of this new sparkle inside me. With a quarter of pregnancies ending in miscarriage in the first trimester, I clung to the happier end of the odds hoping I'd be lucky, but knowing it was out of my control. Suddenly I had an inkling of just how wretched the loss of something so fledging would be.

Miscarriage is unforgiving in every way for those who experience it. I hadn't realised just how unforgiving it was until I went to see a close friend who, a few days before my visit, had messaged me to say she'd lost her baby. The afternoon I spent with her gave me the briefest insight into the impact miscarriage has, not only on a woman's mental state, but also how arduous it can be on a woman's body. I'd never truly grasped the fact that to miscarry is not a contained physical experience, like the breaking of a bone. She hadn't 'miscarried' in the past tense; she was 'miscarrying' right there as we sat on her sofa, eating doughnuts, talking and crying. Her emotional pain I was expecting, but rather naively, her physical pain – the cramps that would suddenly surge and interrupt her speech as she took a breath to gather herself – I was not. As I left her and headed home, I felt honoured that she had trusted me with such rawness and let me bear witness to such an intimate experience. Miscarriage surrounds us far more than we'd imagine. While some women may bleed and cramp for a day or two, for others, their miscarriage may mean several days or even weeks of dealing with a painful and extremely physical legacy which in some cases ends in a necessary medical procedure. There will be women right now in the supermarket, going to work and picking up kids from school who are miscarrying. They have no choice. The world still turns even though the little life inside them no longer does. And once again, I marvel at female fortitude.

Late miscarriage (happening between 12 and 24 weeks) is thankfully much less common, but obviously still sometimes sadly happens. This unbelievably tragic loss is painfully compounded by the fact that at this point, women must labour their no longer living child. Before my mum had my sister and me, she miscarried a baby at 19 weeks – around halfway through the pregnancy. Growing up, I'd always known about the 'first baby', but I was in my late 20s before we had a proper conversation about what she'd gone through. The devastation and trauma she experienced birthing a silent child is too sad for me to comprehend. It was the early 1970s, and my parents were living in Hong Kong. Once they were told that the baby was no longer living, the birth process was started, but things progressed slowly. As night fell, my mum sent my dad home, but once he'd left, things accelerated rapidly, leaving my mother, a 25-year-old first-time mum, thousands of miles away from home, to labour her baby alone. Nowadays, after the birth of a child born sleeping, a woman would be offered the chance to see them, but in those days, the babies were taken straight away. Afterwards, a doctor told my mum that her baby girl had looked completely perfect and his best guess was that the child may have had a weak heart and simply couldn't cope with a fever my mum had been suffering from. The birth had happened in a Catholic hospital where the wards were staffed by nuns as well as nurses. Before my mum left for home, one of the nuns told her that she'd given the child a Catholic name before baptising her, meaning my mother would always have an angel in heaven. I asked my mum how, as a non-religious person, she'd felt about that. She said, 'I didn't want an angel in heaven. I wanted my baby. Here.'

Miscarriage and late miscarriage are, even now, rarely discussed openly, but over 40 years ago, I can only imagine the deafening silence that engulfed my mum. I'm sure my dad did his best to comfort her, but as a man who comes from a generation where male emotion was actively discouraged, my heart breaks as I imagine my mother leaving hospital and trying to piece herself back together. There are millions of women like her, some now grandmothers, who've lived many full and busy years but who carry the loss of their babies who never came home.

During my early days of pregnancy, I would tell myself not

to invest too much – 'Hopefully optimistic, hopefully optimistic,' I would repeat in my head. But it became impossible. Within a day of seeing that positive test result, I was totally seduced by the notion of this child. I started to build a new future in my head. Within a week of finding out, I was researching names and wondering if the babe would prefer a bunny rabbit cuddly toy or the more punky choice of cuddly octopus. As the days totted up, this future I'd created inevitably became more and more tangible – the thought of it suddenly just 'not being' became unthinkable.

We are all, of course, familiar with the magic 12-week mark at which many people wait to share the news of their baby. The idea being that by this point, you've had your first scan, so you know that there's a healthy foetus in there and the risk of miscarrying now significantly reduces. Phil wanted to do exactly this. He was still adjusting to the pregnancy and, while 'hopefully optimistic', was worried about sharing any news when the little sparkle inside me was still so fragile. Having found out very early on that I was pregnant, sticking to this 'rule' would mean over two more months of zipping it. To me, it felt impossible. I'm not suggesting that we all Facebook Live our baby news before the wee on the pregnancy test is dry, but I do think that if you feel like you want to share your news with those you love, don't feel pressured to complete that arbitrary 12 weeks of silence.

For starters, I wanted to talk about being pregnant endlessly. While Phil could provide a certain amount of interested ears (two), I craved the thoughts and experiences of other women who had lived it or were currently living it. All my previously documented ambivalence towards having a child had evaporated. I gleefully cannonballed into an ocean of pregnancy chat and decided I would happily float around in it for the foreseeable. I spent my days absorbing everything I possibly could about being pregnant. I listened to any podcast that had 'mum' in the title, and if it had 'placenta encapsulation' in the episode description, then so much the better. For the first time, I formed opinions on YouTube vloggers (big fan of a jump cut, but anyone who says, 'Hi guyssss,' while doing a head tilt is immediately downgraded). I read threads on Mumsnet from 2002, where women pregnant 16 years ago spoke about due dates of children who would now be old enough to purchase crossbows. If I had any cravings early on, it was for information. I felt it would prepare me for what was to come, whatever that may be. All these online resources from strangers were incredibly helpful, but what I really wanted to do was talk to someone I knew.

If anything went wrong in the first few months, I was very aware that I would need my favourite people around me, so why wouldn't I want to tell them now? But Phil's fears were still very real. Not yet, Ellie. I knew his reticence came from a place of love and protection, so begrudgingly accepted his position but like a child asking, 'Are we nearly there yet?', every day I'd ask him, 'Can I tell my mum yet?'.

I was so excited about the idea of telling my parents. I kept dreaming up all these elaborate ways to share the news with them via fun videos, poems or brilliant puns based around it nearly being Easter (hatching soon, eggciting news, eggcellent work – OK, mostly just egg puns but still top stuff). I loved the idea that they would be the first people to know this precious, life-affirming announcement. What an honour. What a moment. Except they weren't the first to know because along the way, you end up having to tell all sorts of total strangers about your early pregnancy. For example, and in no particular order, I told:

1) My GP.
2) A community midwife.
3) Multiple medical receptionists – one of whom, after hearing me ask to book in another midwife appointment, asked, 'Date of birth?', to which I replied, 'I don't know, I haven't had the baby yet', to which she said, 'No, *your* date of birth'.
4) Various yoga teachers at a studio I signed up to because it seemed like something a glamorous pregnant person would do. Turns out, however, that this pregnant lady is as flexible as a steak knife, and finds other people breathing loudly nearby more irritating than a yeast infection. Seriously – people in those classes are just in it for the competitive exhaling. And don't get me started on the 'restorative' session I went to. God knows why I had to inform the teacher that I was up the duff, bearing in mind all the class involved was lying on the floor in the dark under a blanket that could have done with a bit of Febreze. The most high-octane it got was when the bloke running the class bent down to adjust my head position, and in doing so, his big toe acciden-tally caressed my shoulder. The biggest threat to my foetus in that room was the teacher's lack of access to some nail clippers.
5) Carol Vorderman. Yes, maths whizz, national treasure and two-time winner of Rear of the Year. I was filming a TV show where a group of people off the telly go out for dinner and play silly games. Whoever loses has

to pay for the whole meal, so everyone is encouraged to be decadent little rats, forcing the loser to max out their BA Avios Amex card. So here we are; me, Vorders, Rylan Clark-Neal and Anton du Beke. A classic combo, I think you'll agree. The waitress goes round the table asking for orders. Everyone's going to town. Vorders is on the champagne, Rylan's racking up the martinis and then it gets to me, and I pipe up with, 'A Diet Coke, please.' Immediately, CV is looking at me like a great white circling a sea lion with one flipper. When I ask for my steak to be cooked well-done, the attack is inevitable. The cameras stop rolling as we reset for the next section of the show, and Carol asks me across the table if I might be pregnant. I stare at her. I had a cover story all worked out – I was on a strict health regime implemented by an imaginary and extremely fierce personal trainer called Magdalena. But, goddammit, Carol's power is magnetic. My defences are useless against her enchanting sorcery. I give her an almost imperceptible nod. She quietly squeals. The night unfolds, I don't have to pay the bill, and, long story short, Carol is a very hands-on godmother and we summer together in Mustique.

The not-drinking-alcohol-bit in the secret 12 weeks is such an annoying giveaway. If you can possibly time your pregnancy so you go through that bit during 'Dry January', then I'd heartily recommend it. You can easily span it out into February, too, saying that after a month off the sauce, you're just really vibing Capri-Suns right now.

I went to multiple social events while covertly with child, and for obvious reasons, refused booze at all of them. On at least three other occasions, people noted my drink refusal and asked outright if I was pregnant. Now, while I had embraced Vorders' quizzing - she's a cultural icon after all and has earned the right to ask anyone anything she bloody well likes - the other random strangers questioning the contents of my womb made me feel incredibly uncomfortable. Every time it happened, I had to trot out one of my awful lies, which was then always subject to Emily Maitlis-style questioning to test its robustness. Listen up, dudes – if a woman isn't drinking because she says that she's on antibiotics (a classic), is driving (she doesn't own a car) or has a scary PT called Magdalena, please just accept the blatant fib and move on. If she wanted to tell you her news, regardless of whether you're a complete stranger, a vague acquaintance or her best friend of 20 years, then she would have told you. As soon as she waves away the Proseck, bury your suspicion, and when she does eventually reveal her pregnancy *when she is ready to reveal it to you*, then and *only then* can you storm in with a big fat, 'I KNEW IT!', punch the air and go home to write in your diary about your incredible intuition.

(I remember moaning to a friend – who I'll call Mandy – about the stories I had to concoct when secretly pregnant and how by the end of it, I'd actually started to just accept glasses of wine and pretend to drink them. Mandy who used to be a bit of a wild child, looked at me with zero sympathy and said, 'You think pretending to drink when pregnant is hard – at least you didn't have to pretend to snort cocaine'. She said she had to sort of blow it away, like crumbs off a chopping board.)

To make things worse, I really, really wanted to drink the booze. All the booze. Various mums had said to me that I wouldn't fancy alcohol if I ever got pregnant. That turned out to be bullshit. If people ask me if I had any cravings during pregnancy, I always say, 'Yes, for two things: Pinot and Grigio.' I had the body of a pregnant woman but the booze lust of a fresher on their first trip to Vodka Revolution. Having a tipple or two was a big part of my life in ways I hadn't really clocked before it was taken away.

For instance, my husband and I have zero in common. He likes watching political satire, I like watching *The Real Housewives of . . . Anywhere in America Where Beautiful Women Have Too Many Mimosas and Argue at a Friend's Swimwear Launch*. He studies books called things like *Croatia: A Nation Forged in War*. One of my favourite reads of last year was *Open Book*, the autobiography of 90s pop darling Jessica Simpson (FYI, it's a belter).

His job as a journalist is to accurately report on world events without allowing his opinions to colour the facts. My job involves lying, exaggerating and aggressively hammering home my opinions to make strangers laugh.

We are total opposites, aside from two things that we have to unite us. Those things are:

1) Enjoying each other's company.

2) Enjoying each other's company during boozy evenings.

That's what we have. That's what we are. Our little bursts of over-indulging have united us from the start. Our date nights have and remain to be a joyous greedy affair of cocktails and scoffing. It's our hobby. It's our hedonism. And hedonism is not a fun spectator sport. Watching your favourite person knock back an Argentinian Malbec while you nurse a sparkling water? DULLSVILLE. My husband had previously said that if we did ever have a baby, then he would give up drinking with me in a show of solidarity. A lovely notion until the hypothetical pregnancy became an actual pregnancy where-upon he updated his policy to 'drinking for three'. This made me want to both laugh and, more keenly, kick him in the 'nads.

So it was, fittingly, a booze-related incident that made me realise the different ways in which the pregnant person and their partner experience pregnancy. It was Easter Sunday, and we had my family round for lunch. I was about eight weeks preggo and had still only told two of my friends, some NHS workers, a handful of yogis and Carol Vorderman. This was the day I wanted to use all my great egg jokes as a lovely way to reveal the baby news to my nearest and dearest. However, Phil was still not up for letting the foetal cat out of the uterine bag and asked if we could just keep it quiet for a little longer, so I sucked up my eggstraordinary plans and kept it zipped.

My family arrived, and, as we all stood gossiping in the kitchen, Phil made everyone a Buck's Fizz, including me. Clever, I thought – what a sneaky little bugger. My parents and sister drifted into the other room, and Phil and I found ourselves alone in the kitchen. I quietly congratulated him on his cunning undercover bluff. He looked at me blankly. I said, 'You know, because you've made me a drink.' Silence. Staring. And then the penny finally dropped.

'Oh shit!' he said. 'I forgot you were pregnant!' Insert face palm emoji.

For me, this kid was always at the forefront of my mind. At eight weeks, I was already a mother. Of course I was. It was in me. It *was* me. For Phil, and perhaps other non-gestating other halves, the child was there, but hidden at the back of their mind, like a forgotten tin of evaporated milk lurking in the shadows of a cupboard.

Easter lunch was delicious (a controversial turkey roast dinner – what can I say, I like to sow discord). Cooking and clearing up for eight people was enough to completely exhaust me, and I was annoyed that Phil hadn't done more. Once my family left, I told him so, and he looked a bit confused. It turned out that along with forgetting we had begot new life, he also had zero idea that the first few months of pregnancy are often accompanied with a crushing weariness. Oh, come on, mate. This is pregnancy 101. I was permanently knackered. As a self-employed person, I was lucky to be able to nap in the day (sometimes multiple times) but my word, I felt for the women who don't have that option. Or the even more horrific prospect of being up the duff while also having another spawn to look after.

Phil's two black marks for the day, while irritating at the time, gave me useful leverage in my negotiations. Essentially, my pitch went like this: 'You forgot about me carrying your child and also didn't load the dishwasher; therefore, I now get to tell my mum and dad.'

Scared by the angry, shattered, hormonal lady who had a few days earlier cried in the street because she'd seen 'a really good cat', he relented. It was agreed. We would inform the parents.

We went with Phil's first. I hatched a plan that we should do it over Skype and go for a visual gag using a prop. I've never included prop comedy in my act before, but I figured this was as good a time as ever to branch out.

We settled on a skit involving a 'bun in oven' joke which would have worked better had either of us actually bothered to go out and buy a bun. Instead, we improvised with a Jus-Rol croissant that had been in our freezer for two or three years.

We whacked it in the oven and called them. It was morning here and evening there. As they sat on their sofa talking about how chilly the weather was in Sydney (a frosty 17 degrees Celsius, enough to make my father-in-law wear gloves indoors) Phil and I began our performance.

Phil: Ellie . . . can you . . . can you smell that?

Ellie: What? *dramatic sniffing* Ohh. Yes. Yes, Phil, I can smell something, what is that?

Phil: Oh I don't know . . . it's . . . it's like something's been left in the oven . . .

Ellie: Oh no . . . we'd better go and check what it is . . .
           iPad zooms in on the oven door, which I open
           Look Phil – there is SOMETHING. IN THE OVEN.

<SILENCE>

Phil's mum: . . . What is that? *peers closely at screen* Is that . . . is that a croissant?

Phil: No, mum. I think it's a BUN.

Phil's mum: Oh. *More peering* Looks like a croissant from here . . . our picture isn't very clear, shall we switch to the laptop?

After a few more loud assurances that the croissant was definitely not a croissant, they finally understood. They were delighted. So the day that would mark the start of their life as grandparents would also mark the day I retired from the props comedy circuit. Bittersweet.

(Phil's mum would later tell us that the day before we told her our news, a large, unusual bird had visited her Sydney garden. She'd even taken a photo because it was so unusual. She showed us the picture in question, and there was no denying that it looked like a big stork. She's Catholic and believes that it was a sign from the heavens that she was to become a grandmother. Whatever your view on God, you have to admit that a massive flipping stork is a much clearer message than a small frozen pastry.)

A couple of days later, I rocked up to my parents' in Essex for dinner. Phil was working and was happy for me to go and tell my parents solo. At first, I was a little sad he wouldn't be there, but when I clocked that it meant I would have 100% of the attention, the youngest-child in me did a silent, 'Get in!', coupled with an Andy Murray-esque clenched fist.

I jumped on the train from London and walked up the hill from the local train station to my childhood home. I rang the weird ye olde pull handle iron doorbell that has absolutely no place being on a 1970s suburban three-bed. Mum opened the front door wearing her apron and ushered me in. I stood in the hallway, taking off my coat and shoes while she headed back into the kitchen. As always, Radio 2 was playing, and the surfaces were strewn with pots, spoons and strange implements I'd never seen outside of a JML infomercial.

My mother makes truly beautiful food. She is an excellent, interesting cook who can whip up a meal for 12 out of nothing more than a can of chickpeas and a kiwi. But my god, she destroys the place. Like hurricane levels of destruction. Her Christmas dinner is a thing of dreams but walk into the kitchen afterwards, and you'd think there'd been some kind of culinary police raid.

I said yes to her offer of tea, and as she filled the kettle I said, 'Oh Mum, I need to show you my new badge . . .' She turned around, and I pointed to a Transport for London 'Baby on Board' badge that's meant to make strangers give their bus seat to gestating whales. She stared at it. There was a pause. She said: '. . . No, there isn't?'. I nodded that there was. 'Oh darling!' she said as she pulled me in for a huge cuddle, smothering me in a mother's love and a grubby pinny.

Through happy tears, she told me how overjoyed she was, and how very, very clever I was (which made me question why I worked so hard for my A Levels if all I had to do to be told I was clever was have a contraception-free shag). It was a gorgeous moment that I have squirrelled away in my brain's 'Favourites' album and replay often, usually accompanied by an instrumental version of something by Ed Sheeran.

While she was busy weeping over my intellectual uterus, Dad bustled through the front door. Since he retired a few years back, my father's commitments have gained such momentum his heavily scheduled diary is like that of a minor member of the royal family. His activities include an all-male exercise group called the Keep Fit Club (KFC), a men's rambling troop called WWWW (Wednesday Walking Without Wives), and another group of blokes (acronym pending) who meet up periodically to travel to different branches of Wetherspoons to compare the steak quality ('The Moon and Stars in Romford? Not a patch on The Blue Boar in

Billericay'). He's also a member of the B17 Steam Locomotive Trust, a charity raising funds to build a replica of a particular steam train. The charity is 100% comprised of old dudes who, at their current rate of fundraising (around £15 per century) will need to live until they're 600 years old to see the thing actually built. Even when Dad's in the house, he's still busy. He'll be mowing lawns or trimming hedges, using the pressure washer to blast moss out of the drive or, if in doubt, be sweeping something. He also loves an errand – a trip to the dump, in particular, is a real treat for him.

I don't know if it's just my dad or all men over a certain age, but he is *always* going to the dump. He went to the dump on his 60th birthday. What he is constantly disposing of, I have no idea. (I once wondered if he was a secret serial killer gradually sprinkling the local council tip with body parts, but then realised brutal murder and dismembering would take up valuable time that could be spent selling B17 locomotive zip-up fleeces at the Swindon and Cricklade Railway Steam Gala for a tidy 80p profit, which put my fears to rest).

It turned out that the dump was exactly where he was returning from as I sat in their kitchen, my little badge pinned to my cardy. Mum put the kettle on again (it's rarely off between 7 am–5 pm, after which my mother declares: 'Richard, the sun's over the yardarm – I'll have a Campari and orange, thank you'). Dad took a seat next to me and asked how things were. I said, 'Look at my new badge' (yes, I repeated the gag – give me a break – I was very tired, being pregnant and clever).

He read it aloud, and stared at me, looking astounded before declaring (in a sentence which underlines just how obvious my unmaternal outlook had been to everyone who knew me)

'Well, Ellie, I never thought I'd see the day.' Me too, Dad. Me too.

In line with my need to garner all the information I could humanly gather on pregnancy, birth and this particular person in my womb, I had decided to pay for a private non-invasive prenatal test. This is a blood test that determines the chance of your unborn baby having certain medical conditions.

My main motivations for doing this test were twofold. Firstly, the odds of having a child with these medical conditions increases as you get older and, bearing in mind, I was in my mid-30s and Phil was 107, I believed information was power. Secondly, the test can determine the sex of your child by about 11 weeks, whereas on the NHS, you have to wait till your 20-weeks scan.

I find it extraordinary when people don't want to know what they are having. As an impatient, nosy control freak, the idea of not finding out was preposterous. Keeping it a surprise only works if you have no secret desire. If you are genuinely impartial as to what you've created, then I can imagine it's a thrilling treat to let your partner stare at some miniature genitals in the moments after birth to tell you what you have made. I, however, was not impartial. I cannot overemphasise here just how profoundly, painfully partial I was. I desperately wanted a girl and, not under any circumstance, a stupid boy baby.

Now, if you are reading this as a parent of a stupid boy baby, then firstly, PLEASE DON'T THROW THE BOOK ACROSS THE ROOM – IT MIGHT DAMAGE YOUR PAINTWORK AND I DON'T HAVE TIME FOR ANOTHER TRIP TO THE SMALL CLAIMS COURT

– and secondly, may I take this chance to say that I mean barely any offence to you and yours.

I bet your darling man-child is a wonderful little human. He will undoubtedly go on to contribute huge amounts to society because you will be raising him excellently. I do not hate men. Some of my best husbands are men. My darling attention-stealing nephew is morphing from boyhood into manhood as we speak. Many of my cherished pals have birthed little Adams, lovely sensitive cherubs who will be taught that the inherent advantages they have been born with go hand in hand with a responsibility to advocate for those who are without a penis. These boys are being brought up by some grade-A legends who I know will do everything in their power to ensure that they turn out to be excellent humans and top-notch feminists.

But while I am truly glad to have these little lads in my life, I've always known that I didn't want one living in my house.

I grew up as one of two little girls in a home run by a strong and terrifying mother. All my friends are girls. Female friendships are at the core of my happiness and security. I adore women. I adore *being* a woman. Any daydreams I've ever had about having kids involved little girls with pigtails, or little girls with pretty dresses or little girls sitting on my lap watching me do my make-up while I say wise things like 'Remember, darling, your eyebrows should look like sisters, not twins.' These are, of course, stock 'little girl' images straight from feminist hell, and my daydreams should probably ingest some more Caitlin Moran, but I also stand by them because they are simply a sign of my own happy femininity. To pretend that I didn't look forward to sharing a sense of play around fashion and make-up via my motherhood would suggest I thought my own aesthetic was in some way a weakness or a fault. Of course, my imaginary child shared my interests in my daydream because it was MY daydream. And that's the wonder of fantasies. Everything you want with no tricky strings attached.

So, while my imaginary mothering involved rainbows, plastic clip-on earrings and mini Disney ballgowns, it's safe to say that not one of my daydreams had ever, *ever* involved a tiny person with a tiny scrotum. I had no affection towards the idea of giving birth to a boy.

My desire was Veruca Salt-like in conviction. I. Wanted. A. GIRL. I spent some time examining this violent and bratty desire, and I decided it was essentially down to a lack of imagination and a large portion of vanity.

As a comedian/actor/writer/general show-off for hire, people often assume I have a brain stuffed with new and fresh ideas because, in all my jobs, I create. I create jokes, or characters or the nebulous concept of 'content' for social media. I am undoubtedly a creator, but I've realised that I can't create something out of nothing.

The things I create are always based around *me*. Something that pre-exists. My stand-up material is based around my life. The scripts I've written are all loosely based around my family. My online content is based around mundane domestic things like how great my new spatula is or what weird inanimate object my child has currently taken a fancy to (at time of writing, a carbon monoxide monitor).

I simply do not have the imagination to create something into existence that I haven't already known. And everything about a boy baby was completely out of my realm of experience and, therefore, beyond the powers of my imagination. Fundamentally, I wanted a girl because I was a girl. And the vanity part meant that, if I was honest, I basically wanted to bring up myself. Excellent self-analysis, Ellie. Buy yourself a new sparkly sequin bow.

I knew then, that if I was to be carrying a boy, I would need as much time as possible to prepare, scream, curse, howl at the moon, seek advice from a Tibetan healer and read more Mumsnet forums about Gender Disappointment.

And you'd be surprised by how many forums on the subject are out there. Parents riddled with guilt, knowing they are so lucky to have a healthy child, but also can't shake off their sadness that they never got to meet the little boy or girl that they had cooked up in their heads. Peek online, and you'll find pages and pages of people whispering their secrets to strangers because they know that there's little more shameful than admitting regret or disappointment about one's existing child. Reading these forums made me think that if I was indeed carrying a boy, at least I'd have found a community who would understand my feelings and, more importantly, may be open to some kind of part exchange. But first, I needed to find out what I was dealing with.

So, at ten weeks, Phil and I turned up to a Harley Street clinic where all the staff looked like they'd walked out of a film about Russian models masquerading as sonographers. I had read all the bumpf (of course I bloody had) and knew that before the blood test was undertaken, I would first have an ultrasound 'viability' scan to check that everything looked OK.

Phil and I were ushered into one of the scan rooms, where we were greeted by two exquisite women, one blonde, one brunette, who presumably slotted their baby scanning work around designing their lingerie collections and going on dates with Leo DiCaprio.

The brunette beauty, who seemed to be the more senior of the pair, asked me to lay down on a reclining chair next to a very medical looking set of buttons and screens. She explained that because the baby was so little, if they couldn't see the foetus properly via my stomach, they would have to switch to an internal probe. Personally, this is my favourite of all the probes.

I dutifully hitched up my dress, Russia's Next Top Model squirted some gel on my stomach, and the search for life began. So there I was. Having an ultrasound. Husband sitting next to me, holding my hand. PAH. I'd seen this scenario on screen countless times: women with a belly covered in goo, partner grasping her mitt while they both wait in silence for the stranger in the white coat to say something like 'Mazel tov! It's not a burrito!'.

After a few minutes of baby hunting, Brunette Scanner said she couldn't see clearly enough because my womb was set quite far back *humblebrag*. She was going to switch to the internal probe. A flash of worry must have swept over my face as she made a point of saying that she could definitely see *something*, and that the something was moving, which was a good start.

This was the signal for Blonde Scanner to step into action.

Phil and I watched as she carefully picked up the internal probe and delicately began to clean it. So the scene was now two extremely gorgeous women in a darkened room, one lubing up a dildo-shaped implement, while I lay knickerless on a bed as my husband looked on. Not quite how either of us had imagined our first group scenario, but certainly one to remember.

Probe caressing complete, Blonde Scanner handed the probe to Brunette Scanner, who asked if I was ready. I nodded. *Please be a baby, please be a baby, please be a baby.* Up the probe went, like a ferret up a trouser leg, and instantly, the screen in front of me had a thing on it. A tiny, tiny wriggly thing.

Unmistakably.

A baby.

A twirling, flying, constantly moving little jumping bean. Brunette Scanner sat in silence. She twiddled some knobs, flicked some switches and pressed some buttons, taking measurements and checking figures. She then turned with a smile showing her #ad #influencer perfect teeth, and said, 'Good news. There's one baby with two arms and two legs. Congratulations, you have a viable pregnancy.'

I had imagined this whole scenario countless times. Our first glimpse of the baby and hopefully hearing that everything was OK. How would I feel? How *should* I feel? Would I cry? What if I didn't cry? Would I be scared? Would it be overwhelming? What if it was underwhelming? It turned out what I actually felt in that moment, and something I hadn't really considered as one of the options, was just a very true happiness. Which is unusual for me.

To say I am a glass half empty person isn't fair to pessimists. I am more of a 'What is the point of even filling up the glass – I'll just have to put it in the dishwasher afterwards and then it'll come out streaky 'cos we're low on salt, plus, you know, death awaits us all.' People are surprised when I say this stuff because I appear very outwardly chipper. Even my own mother has trouble believing I am quite such the miserable cow I maintain I am. She can't seem to marry the fact that the chirpy child who used to re-enact *Starlight Express* in its entirety (even though I had no roller-skates, so I had to stick Post-it notes I'd cut into circles onto my Lelli Kelly school shoes) could be quite so dead inside as I claimed to be.

Sometimes I get lovely messages from strangers online who say things like, 'I reckon we could be mates! I'd love to have a night out with you! I bet we'd have an absolute hoot!' I can assure you, dear reader, we wouldn't. Not because of you. *You'd* be great. You'd be charming and vivacious and buy the first round like a good person. But me . . . I'd be nervous and quiet, and I wouldn't like the bar or the drinks and then I'd leave by 8.00 pm because I'm worried about missing the last train (which leaves at 11.30 pm). My general mood at any given moment hovers around the level of 'Eeyore on the way back from a stag do, with 5% phone battery and a mouth ulcer.'

But sitting there, in that ultrasound room, next to my favourite person (Phil, not Brunette Scanner), both of us watching this bouncing, giddy, tiny ball of energy ricocheting around inside me, was a quietly joyful moment. No urge to cry, or feel disbelief or fear. I didn't feel scared. I just felt raw, undiluted, no strings attached happiness. And then we listened to the foetus' ferocious heartbeat, and I heard Phil – a man of balance and restraint – say, 'Oh wow,' which is his equivalent of saying: 'SWEET JESUS, THIS IS MIND-BLOWINGLY-FUCKING-MAGICAL.'

(Later, when I would tell my mum about the scan, she would hear the lightness in my voice and say to me, 'See darling . . . you're not dead inside any more.')

Once the scan was done, I had blood taken – which would

contain the secrets to all the baby's necessary genetic information, including the all-important sex. It's mad clever science (official term). Two weeks later, we were back at the clinic for the results. Once again, Phil and I were led into a little side room, this time accompanied by only one Amazonian goddess (I assumed the others were busy at some kind of Agent Provocateur networking event). She opened my file and told us that the chromosomal checks had all come back with a very low probability of abnormalities.

OK.

She then asked, 'Would you like to know the sex?' ER, JUST A BIT, MATE.

She pulled out a bit of paper and turned it towards me, her finger covering the box that contained the much-coveted information. I double-checked all my details were correct, and once I confirmed that they were, she lifted up her finger and there, in big fat capital letters, was written, FEMALE. I punched the air and screamed, 'Yesssss!' The woman was visibly startled. I assume she is used to a more muted response than someone reacting like they've won £75 on a scratch card.

I was delighted. I was relieved. I'd been trying to prepare myself for it not being my longed-for girl. I knew that, of course, if I were to be carrying a stupid boy baby, that by his 5th or 6th birthday, my resentment would have probably subsided enough for me to look at him directly in the eye. Eventually, I would learn to accept him, in the same way one accepts one's own back fat. It would have been fine. If nothing else, I would have been able to write a new stand-up show about my disappointing boy child called: *Son of a Bitch*. I would have been stoic. I would have gotten used to the idea. I would have undoubtedly loved him completely and totally, my dastardly little lad . . . but now I didn't have to because I HAD MY GIRL!

I walked out of the clinic, wobbly with delight. Reeling with gratitude at the universe and at my husband's lady sperm for giving me such a cracking pair of X chromosomes.

We headed into Soho to grab some brunch. As we sat at a table waiting for our food, Phil snapped a picture from the ultrasound we'd just had done and sent it to his parents with the caption: 'Mum, Dad – meet your granddaughter'.

What a beautiful little croissant.

4

Body

Being pregnant is like watching the Spice Girls movie. You spend half the time thinking it's brilliant, half the time wondering when this atrocity will end and all the time eating snacks.

Aside from a brief period in 1998 when I had a catastrophic pixie hair cut that made me look like a German raver called Joerg, I can't think of another time in life when one will experience such rapid physical change. In just 40 weeks (the same time frame it usually takes me to get through a bottle of hair conditioner), a pregnant body will experience multiple seismic shifts. Some of these things I was expecting, some of them I wasn't, some of them happened to my friends but not me, while other things happened to me but none of my friends. So, in no particular order, please enjoy this bitesize summation of some of the mad stuff a gestating body goes through.

* You swell up like a dead rat floating in a canal. Sure, the bump bit is to be expected, but the fat nose is a real blow.
* Your organs get shoved out the way by your unborn child like a poor person coming too close to a Kardashian. This makes peeing a full-time occupation and breathing as easy as eating a king-sized mattress.

* You get excellent hair. Mine got very thick and bouncy, like one of the well-bred girls from *Made in Chelsea* who's half British, half Cruft's Best in Show winner. My hair also stopped getting greasy. Not having to do all that washing and blow-drying freed up an unexpected amount of time that meant, had I wanted to, I could have learnt the French horn or mastered a Rubik's cube. Instead, I used those bonus hours to watch lots of *RuPaul's Drag Race* while gnawing on a 1kg block of Cathedral City.

* You get lots of that aforementioned excellent hair ALL OVER YOUR BODY. Glossy sprouts all over the shop. My moustache got so luscious around the 20-week mark, I took to wearing it in a chignon.

* Your stomach muscles are ripped apart like a tear 'n' share brioche loaf, never to meet again.

* Your centre of gravity shifts. I'll say that again. Your centre of GRAVITY, as in the UNIVERSAL FORCE, actually SHIFTS, meaning you have to relearn how to MOVE because of the tiny person squatting inside you.

* Blue vagina. No, not the name I go by when trading uranium on the dark web, but what can happen to your lady bits in pregnancy. Extra blood flow can lead to discolouration of the cervix, labia and vagina. The blueish violet hue is known as the 'Chadwick Sign', who was also my favourite character in *Gossip Girl*. I personally have no idea what colour my vagina was, either during pregnancy or even right now, to be honest. We don't see each other much, but thankfully, we have that kind of relationship that means when we do meet again after a hiatus, it's like we've never been apart. However, I like to think that were my vagina to decide she wanted a bit of a rebrand colour-wise, she'd opt for a timeless leopard print.

* Nose bleeds. Before pregnancy, I hadn't had a nosebleed since I was in primary school and Michael Clarke accidentally hit me in the schnoz with a rounders bat during a highly competitive under-eights fixture. And yet, in pregnancy, all the bloody time.

* You can get a strange sensation called carpal tunnel syndrome, which is an irritating tingle in your hand. It's to do with excess fluid collecting and pressing on a nerve. I experienced it a few times and found it maddening. The only thing I found that stopped the feeling was prolonged and excessive waving. How deranged this made me look very much depended on my immediate surroundings:

  * Pregnant lady frantically waving while on a bus? 'How sweet!', passers-by would think. 'Perhaps she's on a pre-baby mini-break to London and is sharing her excitement via this friendly visual greeting! HELLO BACK!'

  * Pregnant lady in Tesco locked in a non-stop meet and greet with a display of tinned tomatoes? Cue a tannoy announcement telling security to head immediately to aisle five to deal with the flapping, rotund woman.

* You can feel very, very sexy. I had a friend who was so hungry for some 'how's your father' with her baby's father that she made them do it in a hospital toilet after a scan. Another told me how their sister, a photographer, was commissioned to capture a home birth on camera for a couple. The labour progressed slowly, and when the couple moved into the birthing pool, their doula suggested the husband start playing with his wife's nipples in order to get

her oxytocin flowing and speed things up a little. Turns out 'birth' isn't the only thing he stimulated as, before long, the pair were doing it. In the pool. While the woman was in labour. And someone was photographing them. So many levels of WTF I don't know where to begin. Surely by that point, vaginal traffic has shifted to a strict one-way system for exiting only? The experience of birth can be described in many different ways: 'incredible', 'empowering' and, for that particular woman, 'horny'.

* The small person living inside you will relax on your stomach like they're the Chief Fun Executive at a tech start-up laying on a bean bag in a 'blue sky creative' session. For me, this unusual pressure on my innards meant digestive acid being squeezed up my gullet like a tube of toothpaste that's been stamped on. It was my first ever run-in with heartburn, and it was quite the punchy surprise, especially after all that Cathedral City.

* You'll need to buy things in bigger sizes. Of course. We all know that. But did you know that may include shoes? Yes – your feet can get wider and longer. That, coupled with the aforementioned 'dead rat in canal' swelling, means you can spend a fair amount of your final trimester attempting to thumb your trotters into some Converse like an ugly sister barking for a shoe horn.

* The fat nose thing again.

You can keep listing them. A hundred physical changes that can happen along the way. Some happen very quickly and seem, at best, completely bananas. Within days of conceiving, my body began to do some things that, with all due respect to the magnificence of human evolution, were fucking stupid.

For example: ma titties. Historically, ma titties had been a very insignificant part of my life. I've never been a fan of them. I've always craved little Parisian boobs. High and perky with tiny nipples the colour of a Body Shop berry lip balm. The type that belong to a girl called Delphine who writes socialist poetry while sucking back on a skinny vape and wearing a silk cami with no bra. She does not give a sheeeet *exhale, shrug, shot of absinthe*.

What I've got, however, is a pair of very unassuming good old Ingerlish bosoms. They sit a little too low and are decorated with large pale nipples you can barely see because they have the pallid colouring of an Edwardian ghost child. The ghost nips face outwards, making them look like they've had an argument about what to watch on Netflix and can't bear to look at one other. To top it all off, my whole breast area seems to be like some cyborg front plate with no nerve endings – it has the sensitivity of a racist grandad.

But within days of finding out I was pregnant, my boobs decided that this, THIS was their big moment. They went from feeling nothing, to feeling *everything*. They became giant orbs of pain. Spheres of anguish. Globes of hurties.

Lying on my front became impossible, putting on bras was torture and even water-spraying them in the shower would make me wince. My tits had turned into millennial snowflakes, whingeing about the price of oat milk and demanding free wind turbines for all.

This was my first inkling that pregnancy permits your body to do things that make you think, 'But what is the *point* of this? How is this weird pregnancy 'side effect' helping me in any way? Mother Nature is a KNOB.' Or the other option: 'Mother Nature is a MAN.' Sure, my boobs would be needed when the baby was here, but that wasn't for 8.5 months, so why were they piping up now? They were like a keen but confused am-dram performer, bursting into the opening scene they aren't actually in, wearing a full sequin jumpsuit declaring that they're ready for their close up.

As well as my boobs, down at the other end of my body another part of my anatomy had decided that now was the time to make themselves known. My pubic bone – previously a nice quiet lad who never gave me any trouble – decided that he'd had enough of hiding in the shadows of my knick knacks and wanted some attention. His time to pounce was when I ran for a train at about two months pregnant. I was imperceptibly pregnant to anyone else, but already a pregnancy hormone called 'relaxin', which helps your joints and muscles loosen to prepare for birth, was pumping around inside me. This meant that, when I dashed to make my train, the tiny ligament that holds the pelvis together under the *mons pubis* (the fatty bit on top of your pubic bone that my friend Bex calls her 'bonnet') overstretched itself due to its new-found elasticity. My baby was still over half a year away from being here and yet, my body had decided that my pelvis needed to get all loosey-goosey right now.

Walking became painful immediately. For a while, I was reduced to shuffling little geisha-like steps. I would get tutted at on pavements for walking too slowly (which just proves you should always be kind to dawdlers – as the saying goes, you never know what's going on under someone else's bonnet). I had what's known as pelvic girdle pain or symphysis pubis dysfunction (PGP/SPD), and some unlucky women get it so badly that by the end of their pregnancy, they have to use crutches or even a wheelchair. No offence, body, but HOW

DOES THAT HELP THE CONTINUED SURVIVAL OF THE HUMAN RACE?

Perhaps it could be seen as nature's way of telling us to take it easy. Once I stopped running for trains or going to the gym and limited my exercise to lifting carbohydrates to mouth height, my PGP thankfully chilled out. It also led to my friend Pete declaring I was experiencing a very nasty 'minjury', so in a way, it was all worth it.

It would, of course, be unthinkable while talking about pregnancy's effect on the female body, if I didn't mention morning sickness – the A-lister of pregnancy symptoms. Thanks to my Lord God and Saviour (Michelle Obama), I was extremely lucky and barely experienced it. The closest I got was a mild but continuous feeling of nausea which could be kept at bay by snacking. Eating and drinking seem to be the main 'solutions' to lots of women's pregnancy nausea, the most famous recommendation being ginger biscuits or flat Coke. I preferred Mini Cheddars, which I would eat on an almost constant basis. Like a chain smoker, but a chain Cheddarer. I wish more feelings of illness could be fixed by grazing – if the cure for hay fever was to eat a 12-pack of Pom-Bears, I'd be dry humping grass clippings all summer long.

This stereotypical little number affects the majority of preg-nant women, with around eight in ten expectant mothers suffering with some form of nausea and vomiting. Many friends have told me stories of puking between meetings, puking in the street, puking in the car, puking in the shower, puking outside McDonald's, puking inside McDonald's but still managing to squeeze in a cheeseburger. To this day, my sister hates going to Old Street Underground station because it reminds her of her pregnancy with my now nine-year-old niece. Many a morning, she emerged from the tube, was sick in a bag, chucked it in a bin and continued to her office.

The science of why morning sickness (or what sometimes is more accurately termed as pregnancy sickness) occurs, is still annoyingly unclear. The general consensus is that it's triggered by a reaction to pregnancy hormones. Other studies have mooted if it's nature's way of protecting a growing baby by ridding the mother of any foodstuff that could contain parasites or toxins that may harm the vulnerable foetus. This theory matches up nicely with the fact that the majority of women will have stopped vomiting by 20 weeks when the baby is more robust and therefore resilient to these potential nasties.

There will, however, be some women reading this now saying, 'Stopped at 20 weeks?! My chundering started when I weed on the pregnancy test and only ended after I delivered my placenta!' This excessive vomiting is known as hyperemesis gravidarum (HG) and can sometimes lead to hospitalisation. In a smart marketing move by HG, it managed to secure Kate Middleton as its poster girl, with the Duchess of Cambridge famously suffering with this debilitating condition while carrying all her children. I don't think it's possible to convey how awful this condition is. Essentially experiencing the effects of a severe stomach bug all day every day, for months on end and, in some cases, the full term of the pregnancy. Dare to suggest a women with HG try a ginger biscuit and expect to be violently assaulted by a lady wearing puke-splattered ASOS maternity dungarees. I cannot imagine the distress felt by women who experience this sort of violent illness, nor the courage of those who risk going through it all again with another pregnancy. It's genuinely heroic. There should be a regular feature on *Good Morning Britain* celebrating mums-to-be with severe sickness. Susanna Reid would throw to Andi Peters live from a house just outside Godalming, where a heavily pregnant woman heaving into a washing-up bowl accepts a bunch of flowers.

Writing about the gruelling pregnancy experiences that some women go through makes me appreciate what a comparatively easy ride I had. Aside from my minjury, the worst it got for me was some pretty nifty backache which meant I took to carrying around a pillow in a bag. On the scale of pregnancy woes it's not exactly the most compelling tale, and I am well aware that a lot of women had and have it considerably harder than Old Tayls.

I do wonder, though, if Old Tayls had been more of a Young Tayls when she was carrying a baby, if things would have been easier. If I'd had kids in my early 20s, would I have had a physically easier pregnancy? Would I still have been a pillow-in-a-bag lady, or would my young springy bones bourne the burden with more ease? Would my bonnet still have broken? Would I still have had a fat nose?

There's certainly a general increase in risks for pregnant women over 35 which don't make for fun reading. We're talking high blood pressure, pre-eclampsia, not to mention increased risk of complications during birth. But with women aged over 40 now having more babies than women under 20, one hopes that 'specialist' care needed for older mothers is getting better and more refined as increasing amounts of women wait to start their family.

One thing I do know is that even if it were the case that my 20-something body may have been better prepared to deal with the challenge of pregnancy, I'm not sure my 20-something brain would have done so well with the actual looking after of the baby. And that section lasts considerably longer than nine months. Sure, if 20-year-old Ellie got pregnant, she may have been able to sprint to all her maternity appointments and achieve a 5km personal best while in early labour, but 20-year-old Ellie also had thousands of pounds of debt and a bloodstream permanently riddled with pineapple Bacardi Breezer. If carrying a pillow in a bag and having a broken bonnet is the price I paid for waiting a bit longer to have a child, then it was the right choice.

5

Work

As I headed into the second trimester, my thoughts turned from poetic musings on the sublime circle of life to more practical concerns like how I was going to pay for all the things this kid would need, like a house and a pram and all of those chicken nuggets. I became concerned about people from work finding out about my pregnancy and withdrawing job offers because I was an insurance liability, or no longer had the right 'look'. 'End of career' type thoughts began circling in my head like planes in a holding pattern. And for once, my worries weren't irrational.

I don't think I've known any female friends who haven't had some concerns about their employment once they found out they were pregnant. I know one woman who felt compelled to keep the news of her pregnancy quiet, throwing up in secret for months specifically in order to be considered for a promotion that she knew would unlikely be given to an 'openly' pregnant woman. I know another who kept her news to herself to make sure she was granted her full bonus. I know a female actor who landed a part in a major TV show, only to be told that she was no longer right for the role because she wouldn't have the physical agility required now she was pregnant (the character was a desk-based police officer).

The threat to the employment of pregnant women and new mothers is a very real one.

I decided that it was time to see where I stood, so arranged a meeting with my stereotypically kick-ass agent to break the news of the growing babe inside me. I girded myself for predictions of a future of rack and ruin, and a new career as a barista. Fortunately, my agent is less dramatic than I am. She gave me her warmest congratulations and a huge smile before switching gears. She looked at me sternly. 'Oh god,' I thought, 'Here it comes – she's going to start suggesting which branch of Costa I should apply to. I've worked so hard to build up my comedy career. I'm not ready to give it all up – even for free Mint Choc Chip Frostinos and a giant custard cream.'

What she actually said was: 'We don't have to tell anyone until you feel comfortable. Regardless of whether a job is something that's already locked in or something new that comes along, as far as I'm concerned, you'll be turning up and doing the work in exactly the same way you usually would, but you just happen to be pregnant. It's no one's business apart from yours. You have no reason to worry.'

What. A. Boss. In an entertainment industry with zero job security, where 'talent' is as disposable as a used Styrofoam kebab box, I felt hugely relieved she was so firmly in my corner.

And, as it turned out, gestating Ellie had one of the most successful periods in her career. I'd whispered a secret little aim to myself and the universe at the beginning of the year in an uncharacteristic moment of self belief and overt ambition. It was thus: *low rumbling drumroll and lots of reverb* 'I, Eleanor Jane Taylor of Essex, first of her name, Mother of

Cheddars, would like to host hit BBC show *Live at the Apollo* and record my own Netflix stand-up special. Kind regards, XOXO.'

And I bloody well did both. While I was bloody well up t'duff.

I found out I'd been offered both of these jobs around the same time, and I knew they would require a lot of hard work. So that is what I did. I did countless tester gigs in London, trying out material, rewriting my jokes and then performing again to perfect both of the different 30-minute sets that each job required.

It was summer, and it was the kind of hot that London is not built for. I was gigging sometimes two or three times a night and I can conjure up countless images of standing on stage wearing one of only two summer dresses that would fit over my ever-expanding gut. Night after night, I would flog my wares, staring out into dark boiling comedy clubs full of hot faces, both me and the audience covered in an icing of sweat and grime.

It was hard. I was exhausted in every sense. I felt the weight of both these high stakes jobs firmly on my shoulders, and my shoulders alone. And yet, at the same time, I have never enjoyed being a comedian more. Being up on stage while visibly pregnant, which turned into very pregnant, which turned into, 'Bloody hell love, sit down, you're making us nervous,' was one of the most (strap in for a cliche) empowering things I have experienced professionally, personally, physically and mentally.

My inner critic can be a truly horrid little mean girl. She whispers my various failings and flaws over and over like a Spotify playlist on shuffle. But when pregnant, the voice became infinitely kinder. It was as though knowing I was to become a mother made it acceptable for me to mother myself. End of incredible self-analysis.

This new voice was kind. It mollycoddled and patronised me in just the right way. It had morphed from a bitchy pinched-faced cheerleader called Samantha, into a rosy-cheeked portly dinner lady called Mrs Bishop (disclaimer – there was a rosy-cheeked portly dinner lady at my primary school called Mrs Bishop. Told you I'm not creative). For the first time that I could remember, I would congratulate myself. Rather than the usual self-loathing and despair that follows a bad gig, Mrs Bishop would instead tell me, 'Don't you worry, you tried your best, we all have bad days at the office. Why don't you go home via the corner shop and treat yourself to some beefy Monster Munch? Tell you what, my darling, make it a Grab Bag. You're working very hard.'

Night after night, I dragged my wider than usual arse around London, stood on stage and did my best. And the next day I would get up, work on my set and head out to start the process again. As well as kindness to myself, I felt an objective pride and appreciation in my body that I hadn't experienced before. I had drunk the 'pregnant women are amazing' Kool-Aid, and in lieu of access to a vodka and Diet Coke, I'd found it so delicious it became my tipple of choice.

My bum didn't fit into our dining room chairs anymore, and I was experiencing chub rub on my inner thighs that meant I had to wear cycling shorts to keep the two gals apart, but for the first time in my life, I truly appreciated my body's capabilities. I watched, almost as an outsider, as my body grew and changed. I felt so proud of it. I kept a diary during my pregnancy, and almost every entry mentions how incredible it was that my body was just getting on and making this baby, this complete new human, and yet I can still do everything else I usually do. In return, all my body asked from me was a few extra snacks, access to a pillow and some thigh lube.

The Netflix special came first. It was recording in Canada at the Just For Laughs comedy festival in Montreal. Due to work perks, I flew business class, which was both brilliant and extremely irritating. It was brilliant because I had a flatbed upon which to rest my uni-thigh, a quality pair of free socks and a nice cabin crew who kept calling me Madame Taylerrrr. It was irritating, however, because I think we all know that if someone else is paying for you to fly in the pointy end of the plane, unless you can post a selfie drinking a glass of champagne accompanied by a smug prick comment about how 'someone has to do it' then you may as well be on a Megabus.

I landed first thing in the morning and checked into my hotel. I headed up to my room, wheeled in my suitcase and my bump and then collapsed in an armchair. I suddenly felt very, very far away from home and strangely physically vulnerable. For someone who is tall, robust and pretty fit, this was a new feeling.

As my pregnancy had progressed, I had started to value my health and my very existence much more than usual. This sounds a bit mad so let me give you an example. Normally I am blasé when it comes to crossing roads. A cursory look both ways, and I'll happily step off the pavement, confident that at any point, I can hold up my all-powerful and graceful palm and instantly halt any oncoming vehicles.

On one of my first dates with Phil, I made a classic Ellie attempt at a road cross, darting in front of some hefty London traffic and making my way to the other side, narrowly missing a speeding car. Phil waited until the stampede of vehicles stopped and followed after me, at which point a black cab driver pulled up next to us and yelled, 'Teach her how to cross the road, mate.' Leaving the problematic point of a random man telling another random man to control his woman aside, it's a shining example of my lackadaisical attitude to staying alive.

But now, my own life had become much more valuable because of what I was carrying. I was like a delivery driver who'd found out that one of the parcels in their van is addressed to them. Immediately the idea of lobbing the package in next door's bin becomes much less attractive. I became physically much more considered. It was so engrained in my brain to walk carefully while pregnant that for a good year after I gave birth, I would still be in the habit of gingerly tiptoeing over the snake pit of cabling in TV studios like I was walking over actual snakes.

Sitting in that hotel room in Montreal, I felt out of my depth. I was responsible for this tiny girl in my tummy, and I had knowingly travelled halfway around the world alone. What if something happened to me? The amount of stress I was to experience over the next few days as adrenaline surged through my body while recording this huge gig couldn't possibly be good for this growing creature. What was I thinking? I was an awful, negligent mother already, who was clearly going to give birth to a stressed, shrivelled little vole.

As luck would have it, my inner kindly dinner lady Mrs Bishop took this moment to start gently whispering in my ear. She told me everything was fine, I was just tired and jet-lagged, and why didn't I go down to the breakfast buffet?

Who was I to argue with Mrs B? So off I went. I enjoyed breakfast so much that I went straight from the buffet to a pancake house for brunch, where I ate a stack of pancakes (because if you're in a place that has a foodstuff in the title and you order anything other than that foodstuff, then you are a psychopath. I'm looking at you, 'I'll have the Pollo Pesto in a Pizza Express.' You disgust me).

The Netflix recording was a few nights later, and thanks to gorgeous audiences and my sheer bloody-mindedness, the show went well. Much better than I could ever have hoped for. I flew home, and then before I knew it, I was heading to London's Eventim Apollo to host *Live at the Apollo*.

I was excited. I felt really good. I knew I had friends and family in the audience, and, more importantly, I knew I had an absolutely banging outfit sorted. I am not a subtle dresser at the best of times – I love kitsch details, bright colours and clashing prints. I've been called many things in my time, but 'chic' has never been one of them.

Tonight was no exception. My stylist Brit had found me an excellent and inappropriately short, skintight black dress covered in diamanté studs. I teamed it with huge silver shoes and some enormous diamanté earrings in the shape of stars. Whichever way my spherical form turned, I caught the light and sparkled. I was a disco ball on legs.

The irony was, I would never have dreamed of wearing something so clingy when not pregnant. I would have felt far too self-conscious of bra overhang or having a stomach that dared to suggest I like Pret baguettes. And yet, when I was swollen with child, I dressed like a 16-year-old girl armed with a Missguided voucher and a hot date down the skate park.

If it wasn't lycra, and almost constricting my breath, I wasn't interested. One of my favourite maternity outfits was a snakeskin dress that made me look like a python digesting a small pig. In tabloid parlance, I was 'pouring my curves' into clothes without a whiff of self-scrutiny for the first time since I was a child. My skin was being stretched to its limits, and it felt like something to be celebrated. I viewed my fullness as an objectively good thing in its entirety. My 'fat hierarchy' had been torn down. Previously, I would have judged and rated myself in anatomical chunks, for example:

Full butt + jubbly boobs = v. good.
Full upper arms + jubbly muffin top = v. bad.
But now, in every sense, I was just one singular giant unit.
Abundant pregnant lady = SENSATIONAL.

So, at seven months pregnant, I went out on stage in four-inch heels and a snatch-grazing hemline to host the UK's biggest televised stand-up show. As always, with important gigs, the best part of the job is when it's over. My favourite memory of that evening is wishing the audience goodnight, and me and my bump-sidekick walking through an unnecessary amount of dry ice as the huge sign for the show lowered behind us. Done.

The next morning, I posted a photo on Instagram of me in my outfit, standing outside my dressing room. It was in this photo that I finally mastered how to pose as a pregnant woman. A seminal moment. Your natural instinct is to cup your arm *around* your bump, but that always means your hand is near your vagina. And it's even worse if you do one of those couples photos where your partner stands behind you and also does an arm cup. DON'T. It looks like they're about to attempt a pelvic exam. Place your hand on *top* of the bump. Much better.

I accompanied the Instagram post with this, in hindsight, far too lengthy caption:

Last night, I hosted Live at The Apollo. *It was always going to be a special night but doing it as a visibly pregnant woman felt particularly important to me.*

When I first found out I was up the duff I had concerns that as a self-employed bona fide hustler, the moment work people found out I was preggo they'd drop me cos they'd be unwilling to employ an incubator. But you know what – I got lucky. Turns out all the people & companies I work for & with, have been more supportive than I ever anticipated.

But not every woman is as fortunate. 54,000 women a year in the UK are made redundant or forced out of their jobs purely because they're pregnant (stats from the Equality & Human Rights Commission). 54,000.

It makes me so angry. We all only got here 'cause a nice lady gave us the short term rental of her uterus. I think people ignore that sometimes, too busy rolling their eyes in a haze of 'Claire's on maternity leave AGAIN'. Women having kids is literally life, babes. It's what your mum did. Would you want her to have been moaned about and sidelined when she was carrying you? Course not. You'd want her to have been treated kindly and offered a chair and a biscuit.

Pregnant women who work deserve so much more than being forced out or down. Sure, we may be a bit slower, we may wee 67,386 times a day, we may not be able to roll over in bed without the help of a small forklift truck operator called Ian, but we also work harder than ever while going through the trickiest physical change I for one, have ever experienced.

So to all you fellow preggos out there, traipsing into work, through sickness, tiredness, back ache, pelvic girdle bullshit & javelin vagina (yep it's a thing), keep on trucking my nauseous, cankle-riddled, fat-nosed lovelies.

Anything you can do, we can do gestating and in heels.

Now, hopefully you read that and were struck by two things:

1) God, what a great writer. She should do a book.

2) WTaF? 54,000 women a year lose their jobs purely for growing the next generation?

When I first read this statistic from 'Pregnant then Screwed', an amazing organisation that advocates for women who have experienced pregnancy or maternity discrimination, I was shocked, and then I was furious. Lord knows that these stats will have inevitably only increased in the light of the Covid pandemic. The founder of 'Pregnant then Screwed', Joeli Brearley, has written an incredible book by the same name, which is part manifesto and part practical guide to navigating prejudice against working mothers in the UK. With Brearley revealing that a shocking 77% of working mums have experienced some form of discrimination in the workplace, it's an absolute must-read.

The pervasive attitude about pregnant women being, from an employer's perspective, anything from a slight annoyance to a downright problem is so baked into how we think, that even pregnant women talk about *themselves* in this way. We dismiss ourselves and our pregnancy as an unfortunate nuisance. I've heard multiple friends of mine who are expecting a child, especially if it is their second, say how 'guilty' they feel because they'll have to take another stint of maternity leave. Let me just clear this up.

You.

Have.

Nothing.

To.

Feel.

Guilty.

About.

Maternity leave is not you thieving from the till. You are not embezzling from the company accounts or selling the photocopier on eBay. You are making a human. Just as your parents did. Just as everyone's parents did. Even the boss who you don't trust to guard your job while you're on leave. Having a child as a working woman is not, and should never be, something around which to feel any shame, guilt or embarrassment at all. Ever. Regardless of whether you have one kid or five. (Although, if you do have five, and I say this with love, you're fucking nuts.)

Now, I am not the person to get into the ins and outs of employment law (shocking, I know), or arguments about how tricky small businesses may find it when an employee needs to take maternity leave, but I am the person to say that, if you are working with a pregnant woman, do not dare look at her and think that she is, in any way, slacking.

If she's off with sickness, or she leaves early for hospital appointments, she is no less committed to her job. She is doing her regular job *plus* carrying around another life with all the nausea, tiredness and blue-tinted vaginas that her pregnancy may entail. Her occasional absences do not mean she is doing *less* than you; it means she is doing *more*. And you can make her life easier.

Would it be more convenient for her to have the car parking spot closest to the front door, so she has to waddle for a shorter distance? Can you perhaps make that 5 pm meeting a 4 pm one because she's feeling particularly pooped? Can you ask Andrew from Accounts if he'd mind switching to chicken wraps for a bit because his tuna ones risk making her puke on her laptop (again)?

And if you're a pregnant self-employed person, believe me, I know the different sort of stress that brings. You may not be at the whim of a boss or a manager, but you are terrified your clients will all flee unless you're back on that Zoom meeting before they've even clamped the cord.

The point at which a woman decides to stop working before she gives birth, is an emotional decision that is unfortunately often dictated by practical concerns. Wanting time to relax and prepare for the enormous task ahead gets trumped by the fear of 'wasting' weeks of precious maternity leave on days where you are still baby free. Looking back, I should have stopped working a few weeks before I actually did. I put myself under a lot of pressure to do 'just one more job', which inevitably led to another one. And then another. Being self-employed, I did this partly for financial reasons, wanting to make sure I'd swept as much money off the table as I possibly could before I stopped earning for the foreseeable future, but also because I think I feared disappearing. If I could just assert my presence a little more keenly, I thought, then people would remember me for longer. I now look back at jobs I did when heavily pregnant and see a very tired woman essentially waving her hands in the air yelling: 'LOOK AT ME! I'M HERE!

CAN YOU SEE ME? I AM EXTREMELY VISIBLE AND RELEVANT.'

What I really needed at this point was a good talking to by my dinner lady spirit guide, Mrs Bishop. The problem was, I was too busy shouting, 'I will start my maternity leave when the baby crowns and not a moment before!', to hear her gentle advice.

If I had actually stopped to listen, I would have heard her whisper, as I lay on her lap and she gently stroked my hair. 'Now see here, lass,' (she comes from Yorkshire in this section. To set the whole scene, she's sitting on an ancient floral sofa next to some knitting she's put aside). 'You keep accepting jobs when you are very, very pregnant, and I'm not sure it's a good idea. I have a little inkling that when it comes to it, at nearly 39 weeks gone, you might just wish you could put your feet up and spend some time by yourself. So what I would suggest, my darling, is maybe stop work a few weeks earlier. I know you think it's a waste of time, but it won't be sweetheart, I promise. You'll be ever so tired. Your body will have done so much for you and will still have the hardest bit ahead, so the least you can do is give it a few weeks of comfy chairs, iced buns and close access to a toilet because you'll need to wee as often as you blink by that point. Work isn't going anywhere. The universe won't shut up shop because you step back for a few more weeks. You only get to do this bit once. You only get to be full to the brim with your girl, once. So enjoy your last few weeks together. Her kicks as she boots a plate of Battenberg off your tummy. Her hiccups when you have a cold drink. Going swimming, you paddling in the cool pool with her floating inside you like your own little mermaid. The last days of you and her as one. Because before you know it, she'll be here, and she won't be just yours anymore.'

So if that's you reading this right now, heavily pregnant but determined to keep on keeping on, even if it means giving birth on a blanket of Post-its in the stationery cupboard before your 3 pm budget meeting, it's time to summon up your own inner dinner lady to tell you to BLOODY WELL GO HOME.

Bra off, PJs on, feet up. Those are your orders.

6

Gear

Once you hit the third trimester, your focus inevitably needs to shift. Are you eight months pregnant and still staring out of windows, imagining your future life as a mother? Does your time pass with visions of your future perfect angel baby who is only ever wearing a pristine white linen romper and lying on a sheepskin rug while you, well-rested and thin-of-nose, do pilates in a forest? WELL SNAP OUT OF IT, WOMAN. You need to *prepare*. It's time to get all your ducks in a row, and by ducks, I mean birth plan, giant maternity pads and, of course, all the 'stuff' a tiny person the same length as a piece of A4 paper requires. The 'stuff' is crucial and, more importantly, the 'stuff' is bloody expensive.

The problem is, that as new parents, you are going in blind. Of course, you know the basics. You know that the tiny wriggling insurgent inside you is plotting an imminent invasion of your home. You know that if you want to emerge from this siege victorious, then you must assess your armoury and stockpile accordingly. If this is your first child, you will never before have encountered this *particular* kind of dribbly, incontinent enemy. You are unfamiliar with what dastardly tactics it will deploy against you and on what type of terrain it flourishes. The time, therefore, has come to consult more experienced soldiers about what needs to be on your kit list. You create a WhatsApp SOS plea:

'Hi Mum/pal/co-worker, can you send me a list of what you think I need to get before the baby arrives? Thanks!'

I suggest that the very *first* thing you buy once you've hit 'send' on this message is an incredibly sturdy umbrella to huddle underneath before the barrage of replies start pelting down on you. Because they will. Like, huge hailstones made exclusively from links to the John Lewis website and screen grabbed pictures of nasal aspirators. It's only then, as you try to shelter from this oppressive shower of information that you begin to grasp how intense the passionate cult of parenting truly is.

The problem stems from the fact that any existing parent who has made it through the newborn stage is so elated with their own survival that they become evangelical about what 'things' they consider saved them. It's a bit like when I bought a cordless Dyson vacuum cleaner. Yes, it cost the same as a private island in the South Pacific, but the things it could do to a fluff-covered skirting board verged on the erotic. I fell hard for that Dyson. I told everyone that they *must* get that Dyson. I forced a neighbour to take it for a test drive up their stairs so they could appreciate the magnificence of its suction. Now imagine, that instead of wanting to share the feeling of having an exceptionally clean hall runner, the thing you actually want to share centres around salvation of your very soul in the face of a screaming baby.

You have never known more ardent shopping advocates than a mum telling a pregnant woman what she needs to buy.

'SWADDLES!' she will shout in your face. 'These are non-negotiable, you hear me? And not the loose kind you fold yourself, that's pointless – you need velcro – if he looks like he's in a miniature straitjacket, then good, you're doing it right. They. Must. Be. Contained. And for the love of god, make sure you get babygros with zips. Do you hear me? ONLY zips. Not poppers. Poppers are bullshit. Imagine a 3.00 am poonami: it's dark, the wipes are out of reach, you've slept for seven minutes in the last month – do you really want to be fiddling around with poppers? No? Exactly. ZIPS and only zips.' By this point, the mother will be very close to your face, clasping your hand like Jack clung to Rose's at the end of Titanic. 'And promise me,' she'll say, popping with spit, 'PROMISE me, you'll have some Anusol ready for when you get back from the hospital?' Terrified, you promise you will. She nods, unclasps your hand, kisses your bump, sits back down at her till and says, 'That'll be £30.76. Do you have a Nectar card?'

A key problem with all this advice is that much of what you 'need' for a baby is subjective. There'll be people reading the imaginary rant above about swaddles, zips and Anusol and thinking that all three are totally pointless, and instead, the fictional lady should be ranting about the necessity of rocking chairs, scratch mitts and cranial massage. I visited a pregnant friend recently, and she asked me to go through a spreadsheet (yes, spreadsheet) her sister had sent to her, listing all the items she needed to buy. There were 86 separate things listed (some of which included sub-items within them). Of that 86, there were some that I couldn't quibble with – we're talking your pram, car seat, cot. But when it got down to the smaller things, there were at least ten items I thought deeply unnecessary ('Cornflour to use as talcum powder? What is she on about? What's this next one . . . bonnets? Bonnets? I'm sorry, I thought you were having a boy, not an Edwardian. And as for a 'baby wipe warmer' . . . are you pregnant with a tiny diva Mariah Carey?'). There was also another ten I thought were urgently missing ('Where is the white noise machine? And what about olive oil to moisturise the baby, so it stays soft and smells like Italian food? And she hasn't listed earplugs for the hospital – is she insane? Rule one of a labour ward – block those other bitches out').

Every parent's foray into life with a baby is obviously unique, but, at some point, you forget that and begin to assume that your parenting experience is, in fact, 'The Definitive and Only Parenting Experience'. And yet, one person's experience may centre around cornflour, whereas someone else's (mine) may centre around Anusol. And, of course, the same goes for babies, and here comes another lovely truism, but each baby really is different. You often hear that phrase. You will use it yourself, and yet those of us with one child easily return to the default setting that they are the universe's official 'Child Representative'. What works for your child will, of course, work for another because your child is ALL CHILDREN. Nonsense, of course. My friend, the ex-Patsy with twins, is brilliant for reminding me how flawed that assumption is. She had two babies (that's how twins work), born and raised in exactly the same way, and yet one of them took a dummy and one of them refused, one of them liked one particular brand of bottle teat where one preferred another, one is the governor of California and one is Danny DeVito. Small examples of why someone fervently yelling, 'SWADDLES!', in your pregnant face like they're sharing the good word of a very Mumsnet-focused god should be treated with an open mind.

I found the 'getting all the things' part of the final months overwhelming. Some people thoroughly enjoy this process. I know many expectant parents who've delighted in ensuring tiny beautiful wardrobes are filled with tiny beautiful clothes on tiny beautiful hangers. They've revelled in finding rainbow-shaped shelves that will be fitted and stocked with children's books rich in parental nostalgia and empowerment. Joyful evenings are spent sourcing frilly handmade baby smocks from bespoke Parisian sellers on Etsy and commissioning local artists to daub the lyrics of 'You Are My Sunshine' above the hand-crafted cot using gold leaf and harvested colostrum. This, however, was not me.

I was well aware of my ignorance surrounding 'babies' as a specialist subject, but the influx of 'Stuff You Need' lists from friends started to make it very clear it was more than that. I wasn't just ignorant; I was *illiterate*. It's hard to underline how little I knew. I'd barely held a baby. I had no idea how they worked or how to restore factory settings. The basics baffled me. Why was there so much 'vest' chat from my parent friends? Why would a baby need a vest if they were already in a babygro? 'Oh, the vest goes underneath?' I would ask as my sister patiently answered my clueless questions. 'And why are these muslin things such a big deal? Aren't they just expensive tea towels? I might just use tea towels then. I tell you what, 'tea towel' is easier to write on predictive text – my phone keeps changing muslins to Muslims. I know Mamas & Papas is well-stocked, but I don't think they sell whole religious groups. And do I have to get a breast pump? What are these latex pumps as opposed to electric ones? Do I need bottles? You think I do? Even if I hope to breastfeed? Oh right, yes, I suppose I do need them, otherwise, what would I do with the milk I get from the pump . . . and that means I'll need a steriliser too, does it? I can get one that goes in the microwave? OK, I'll do that then . . . oh hang on, we don't have a microwave. Guess we'll have to get one of those as well . . .'

We seemed to need so many things that I maturely decided the best course of action was to shove my head, complete with my fat nose, firmly in the 'child-free' sand. I bought *nothing*. By the time I was 30 weeks pregnant, our entire preparation consisted of a second-hand baby bouncer gifted from my neighbour and one tiny t-shirt emblazoned with 'HAPPY LITTLE VEGEMITE' sent by one of Phil's Australian friends, perfect for a baby due in the depths of a British winter.

I remember a visit to my parents around this time where my mum took a break from destroying the kitchen while making dinner to encourage me to take a peek in my old bedroom. I clambered up the stairs, opened the door and saw the bed covered in freshly laundered hand-me-down baby clothes from my sister's children. Piles and piles of diddy cardigans, those confusing vests and teeny weeny hats. I froze at the doorway as if I'd just spotted a huge nest of spiders as opposed to some neatly folded jumpers from GAP Kids. I backed out of the room, closed the door and left the clothes exactly where they were. When I got home, Mum texted to ask why I hadn't taken them with me. I said I'd just forgotten but the truth was, they scared me. Seeing all those miniature clothes prompted no wondrous swoops of butterflies or giddy squeals of, 'Oh my god! Look how small the feet are!' In their place was, instead, just a slowly rising anxiety.

For as long as I possibly could, I eked out my denial but eventually, whether I liked it or not, I knew I had no option but to enter a proper baby shop to look at proper baby prams.

I braced myself and headed to a shopping mall with this as my sole aim. After walking back and forth past the store like a spy scoping out the best toilet cubicle in which to hide a taser and Lithuanian passport, I finally ventured in. Instantly, I felt uncomfortable. This was a place where 'Other People' belonged, not me. Other People who had families and said things like, 'Yes, the weather was a bit bleak yesterday, but it didn't stop us! We were at the park by 6.30 am – if anything, the torrential rain made eating our packed lunch even more fun!'. This shop wasn't meant for the likes of me, someone so carefree I went out for dinner three times a week and so hip I was considering getting a second ear piercing.

'Right,' I thought, swallowing my strange fear, 'Get a grip. Game face on. You can do this. Prams are what I need . . . where be the prams?' Quickly, though, I discovered I was a goddamn fool, *fool* I tell you, to think I was after just a 'pram'. Turned out what I was *actually* looking for was a 'travel system'. What a cretin. After about 15 minutes reading labels that seemed to be written in Klingon, I walked out of the shop, my heart racing. I went immediately to Starbucks, where I ate a hefty amount of feelings via the medium of chocolate croissants while frantically looking up what the chuff is an Isofix.

It sounds nonsensical, a heavily pregnant woman, happily and deliberately with child, yet seemingly finding the idea of her baby actually being Earth-side too much to contemplate. But it was. It was possible for me to both greedily want my child but also find the mental adjustment of gargantuan (and fast) approaching responsibility a difficult transition. I simply wasn't ready to accept my upcoming 'mother' credentials and all the paraphernalia that came with it. I was halfway between two worlds: still living and enjoying an independent and spontaneous life and at the same time fearfully preparing for (and incubating) the opposite. It felt as though, with every purchase on my 'list', a chunk of my freedom would be hacked away until what was left would be an ugly unfamiliar life I didn't know.

From the disastrous shopping mall day onwards, I treated myself more gently. I looked at the advice I'd been sent by friends of what to buy, and spent a few more weeks sticking to the safety of online shopping, teaching myself fluency in the language of Grobags and next-to-me cots. I decided that I could either spend hours deliberating over which were the best items to buy, signing up to *Which?*, writing pros and cons for each product before cross-referencing my findings with what Rochelle Humes recommended on Instagram OR I could apply the much simpler 'Ellie Taylor Winter Boot' Method. I went with the latter.

The ETWB Method is something I developed a few years ago when agonising over what pair of black heeled boots I should buy. There were so many out there. So many fitted. So many looked good. I was going round and round in circles, not wanting to make the wrong decision on this sizeable seasonal purchase. But in a moment of divine enlightenment, I realised that after I had bought a pair of boots, I would never again consider my decision. They would just be 'my boots'. And if that were the case, why was I bothering with all this initial agony? Why didn't I just find a pair that fitted, buy them, wear them and afterwards move my brainpower onto more important considerations like what really *is* happiness, was the concept of maths created or discovered, and, more importantly, why had I used the word 'amazeballs' so frequently in years 2008–2010?

So that is the method I employed to buy all the baby 'stuff'.

Decided what I wanted, found the first one that met all the criteria, bought it, had a biscuit. And it worked. Pram, car seat, Anusol. Tick, Tick, Tick. And you know what, I really *haven't* considered any of those choices again (aside from the muslins – turns out two or three would have been sufficient as opposed to the 157 I ended up with. But I'll tell you what, my tea towel drawer now overfloweth). Once we started to cross things off the list, the whole process seemed far more manageable and achievable. Soon our living room looked like an Amazon depot, stacked up with parcels of all the baby's things (minus a box of cornflour) and eventually, I even allowed my mum to bring over the clothes my sister had given me.

My bravest moment came at around 38 weeks pregnant, when I was out shopping for nursing bras. This is quite the process in itself. Once in the changing cubicle, the lady doing my fitting passed me something which *she* said was a bra but looked to *me* like some kind of apparatus used to rescue sea mammals from oil spills. I dutifully popped on the strange-giant-double-boob-sling. The cups looked a bit flabby and empty. I told the lady so. She looked at me with pity, like I was a tiny woodland vole about to stroll into the open mouth of a sneaky fox. She told me to make a fist with my hand and then stuff that fist into one of the bra cups. The cup was immediately full. 'Yep,' she said, 'That's how much extra room you'll need when your milk comes in'. That is the kind of underwear sizing I can get on board with.

'What are you? 34D?'

'I'm a two fister, actually. Three, when I'm due on.'

Once the orca hammocks were purchased, I found myself walking past the baby store that had unnerved me so much just a few weeks earlier. But things felt different now. I took a breath and decided that I was going in. As I headed through the doors, I braced myself to feel some kind of mounting trepidation . . . nothing. I tested the waters a little more, going up onto the terrifying pram floor . . . still, I felt at ease. It seemed that knowing we had everything we 'needed' had popped the pressure balloon. Every little decision that I'd made, every baby 'thing' I'd picked, ordered and paid for had chipped away at my mountain of anxiety, leaving barely a raised hillock. What a revolutionary finding – that preparing for a situation is better than ignoring it. I smell a TEDx talk in the works.

I lingered in the baby shop, absorbing and acknowledging a quiet acceptance that this place, filled with bassinets and changing mats, was, for a while at least, my new arena. I even bought something. Not from any of the lists I'd been sent, not an essential, or a wise investment, but just a cuddly toy. My daughter's very first teddy. It felt like a special purchase, steeped in promise. A new paragraph moving things on from the dry practical preparations of furniture assembly, breast pump practising and tumble dryer installation. This silly cuddly elephant, soft and silky in a muted grey with such a kind little face, felt like the acknowledgement of something much, much sweeter. Once home, I went straight up to the room that would very soon be hers, and placed the elephant in the cot. There he sat, waiting for her. A little friend, chosen with such love and hope, ready to welcome her home.

I would like to say that my child and the elephant are now inseparable and that I've even had to buy a spare because her love for him is that wearing, but in the perfect portrayal of how kids have zero regard for romanticism and satisfying narrative arcs, I can report that my daughter has never given, and still could not give, one shiny shit about that little cuddly toy. Zero. Her favourite thing to snuggle up to is a bunny rabbit given to her by the mother of someone I briefly worked with. A lovely gesture by a person I have met twice and who has never met my daughter. And you know what, I think I prefer it this way. I think my daughter is right not to care about that nameless nelly, who now sits ignored on a shelf next to a half-empty bottle of Calpol and a pot of tiny hair-bands. That toy undoubtedly served a heavy purpose – for me, not her. He was bought for 'the idea' of my child, an offering almost, a promise of the connection that I was finally ready to make that day in the smug baby shop. Perhaps when my daughter is a little older, I'll take the elephant down off his abandoned perch, blow the dust off his pristine ears and untouched trunk and tell her the story of how he was the first present mummy ever bought her. And, all being well, she will completely ignore me, throw him on the floor and ask if she can have a Cornetto. Because I think, really, he was always meant just for me. My elephant, not hers. An Elliephant.

7

Prep

Once you have used all your existing parent friends to gather advice and buy more 'stuff' than you can shake a rectal thermometer at, it then becomes paramount to ensure you have access to people who are as clueless (or, preferably, even more clueless) than you. These people will be fellow expectant parents, and they will serve two purposes. Firstly, they will be living in the upside-down world of late pregnancy/the newborn days right alongside you. Secondly, their naivety will occasionally allow you to feel a lovely glow of superiority which will act like balm to your weary stretch-marked spirit.

Like many parents, we decided to source our counterparts via a parenting course. We attended classes run by NCT (which stands for National Children's Ting. I think. No one knows for sure). Fun fact, my Irish friend Brona told me that in Ireland, NCT stands for 'National Car Test', which is what Brits would call an MOT. She had found it very strange when she moved to the UK that, so often, the parents she knew seemed to have made friends while getting their car sorted. Kwik Fit: uniting the sleep-deprived.

While the NCT groups are probably the most well known, there are plenty of alternative prenatal classes out there, called things like 'Bump and Beyond', 'The Birthing Club' and

'What End is What?'. Regardless of the name of the group, the sessions always seem to be held in a Salvation Army church hall on a Thursday night, and will almost certainly be run by a woman called Janet who wears culottes and a lot of Fairtrade jewellery. You will spend much of the evening sitting in a circle staring at another six or seven couples who are staring right back at you. Janet will warmly welcome everybody, explain where to find the tea and coffee station and then get things cracking by asking if anyone knows what a mucus plug is before showing you a Google image that can best be described as harrowing. (A mucus plug is the collection of secretions that seal up a pregnant woman's cervix. Nature's cork if you will. When the unpopping of the cork occurs, it brightens up your knickers in a unique way that Janet told us would look like a 'bloody oyster', at which point all the oysters in the world breathed a sigh of relief, delighted that their sexualised aphrodisiac objectification was finally over.)

You'll probably spend much of the classes trying to pigeon-hole each couple. Who are the cool ones you hope will invite you over for traditional calzone straight from their compost-fuelled pizza oven while playing ironic 70s pop on a gramophone? Who are the funny ones who'll make you howl with laughter while also making you question the calibre of you and your partner's own craic, leading you to hiss at your husband to 'be more vivacious'? Who are the dull ones whose names you can never remember because they have the charisma of a mucus plug and will call their child Ian? You'll be on high alert for the moment that the dud annoying pair reveal themselves, all the while hoping that it isn't, in fact, you. It's a hard line to walk. While I was hopeless on the 'things' the baby needed, on the birth process itself, I felt more informed.

My passion for homework meant I had read multiple books on the subject and watched the film *Knocked Up* at least three times, so it was painful for me as a natural teacher's pet to have to hide my expert knowledge under a bushel. But under a bushel it stayed. As tempting as it was to shoot my hand in the air when Janet asked a question, I knew no one would want to be friends with the woman who kept belting out answers like a montage from University Challenge. 'VENTOUSE!', 'TENS MACHINE!', 'THE MIDWIFE WILL WIPE IT AWAY DISCREETLY!'.

I'd recommend that any new parent attend some kind of prenatal class, be it a private one like we did or a free one hosted by your local hospital. While the teaching may vary, the constant will always be the group of strangers linked by the incredibly commonplace and yet life-altering experience that is looming on your collective horizon. The most satisfying thing I gained from our time with Janet and her culottes was the space it gave my husband to focus on the impending baby. I had been physically experiencing this child for many months now. I'd spent hours talking to female friends about how I was feeling, about my approach to the birth and my hopes for the future of my pelvic floor. For Phil, through biology alone, his experience had been much less involved. Having this weekly opportunity to talk openly in front of other men who were then able to ask questions, that if I'm honest, some of the female partners (me) may have ordinarily laughed at, was incredibly valuable.

Not that Phil hadn't read books. Like me, he'd got stuck in, reading many a manual, but unfortunately, it's fair to say that much of the male-focused literature on pregnancy and birth is as abysmal as you'd imagine. These books adhere to the same sort of gender stereotyping that male grooming products do. We are all familiar with the fundamental science that requires men to avoid using 'lady' shower gel in case some particles of rogue femininity penetrate their robust man pores. The difference between the two options is easy to spot. Feeble lady shower gels have names like 'Hibiscus & Tulip Dew' or 'Sunset Kitten with Cashmere' whereas MALE shower gel is only available in a black bottle in the shape of an axe and will be called something along the lines of 'Carbon Gun Gunk' with the slogan 'Stink like Steak.'

It's this same embarrassing macho road that 'pregnancy for men' books often head down. Rather than talking to men as basic-functioning humans, they make the assumption that all blokes can only compute information if it's delivered in the language of an 80s action movie. The worst offender Phil came across was a manual for dads that focuses on an elaborate Marine metaphor. The father-to-be is the soldier; no man must be left behind, morale of your troop is key etc. If you managed to read that sentence and not roll your eyes, I assume you are either still processing the bloody oyster comment or you are dead. Now, I, of course, understand that the Marine hook is just a gimmick and a way to market a book, but it's incredibly patronising. Its sheer existence annoyed me on my husband's behalf, and it's not often I think 'poor men'. If it were reversed – if a typically 'male' experience was being explained to women via a stereotypically 'female experience', then it would be called out. Plain and simple. On that note, I am pleased to announce the title of my next book: *DIY For Women: How Your Skills in Liquid Eyeliner and Being the Only One to Pick Piles of Stuff Up From the Stairs Can Help You Build Your Own Shed*. Available for pre-order now.

Aside from the top-notch oyster chat and a session where Janet gave each couple a plastic doll wearing a nappy containing a different condiment representing the different types of poo to expect (dijon mustard was featured, if you're wondering), I can't remember many specifics about what we learnt in the classes. The biggest benefit was always going to be the people we would meet. I was there for the humans who would provide us with an instant new parent community – the information we ingested along the way was just a handy bonus. It was a similar situation when my Auntie Pam got divorced and started salsa lessons. Sure, she enjoyed working on her swing step, but once she hit it off with snake-hipped, single Clive while learning a routine to the Ricky Martin classic 'She Bangs', neither of them felt the need to return. Clive was her aim, not the irresistible Latin rhythm. That was me and the parenting classes. They were basically a way to buy some friends. Essentially, we spent £200 on a new WhatsApp group.

Actually, it was *two* new WhatsApp groups. There was a chat for the pregnant women and a separate chat for the 'partners' who, in our boringly hetero case, were all men. I can report that the blokes have had a somewhat minimalist approach to communication – I don't think a message has been sent on the dads' chat for over two years now. It is behaviour that is annoyingly in line with the stereotyping perpetuated by the Marine-based baby book, or maybe it's precisely those kinds of books and attitudes that make men far less likely to share with one another in the first place.

The women's chat, on the other hand, has been buzzing nonstop since inception. Yes, of course, there were inevitable teething problems while we got to grips with the dynamics at play, for instance, I quickly learnt that not everyone was on board with my use of the sushi emoji to refer to vaginas, and that beginning my messages with the greeting, 'Alright schlags', was probably a little too familiar at this stage of our fledging friendship. But those hiccups aside, the group was and still is regularly and comfortingly active for a variety of different reasons. From swapping tips on birth and emotional recovery, trading recipes and birthday present ideas, to haemorrhoid-focused anecdotes that could win The Man Booker prize. Women uniting. Women caring. Women sharing their vulnerability to be met with love, support and a perfectly selected bum grape GIF.

One of the main focuses of prenatal classes is the process of vaginal birth. Many hours will be dedicated to learning about what happens when the process begins, what to expect from contractions and what type of pain relief you may be offered. Janet may teach you some positions that your partner can assist you with during labour or facilitate a group brainstorm about the best snacks to bring to the hospital for the marathon you and your uterus will be undertaking (big shout out to Pringles and Fruittellas).

I found these discussions incredibly interesting. I listened intently, asked many questions and was a very vocal part of the conversation. And yet, always with the hope that I would never have to actually put any of this knowledge into practice because I had a secret weapon. A secret weapon that I suspected would allow me to opt-out of this particular right of womanly (birth canal) passage. That weapon was, drum roll . . . . 'Incredibly Delicate Vaginal Skin'! TADAR! Cue the confetti cannon and male cheerleaders!

I've always had needy skin. As a kid, I was always being

slathered in E45 after another eczema flare-up had turned the inside of my elbows bright red, scratched raw by little fingers trying to find relief. To this day, I will occasionally wake up and find the skin around my eyes has swollen up, making it look like I've been punched. This usually coincides with my lips following suit, becoming inflamed and dry with a thirst that no amount of Vaseline can quench. These face flare-ups often last months at a time. Months spent wearing sunglasses indoors like I'm Anna Wintour, months of avoiding mirrors and apologising to make-up artists who have to try and cover up what I refer to as 'poorly eye'. I have tried all sorts of tests and potions to determine a cause.

Not to be left out, about ten years ago, I started to have issues below deck. Almost overnight, my most intimate skin decided to develop the fragility of Laurence Fox. It was causing me a fair amount of discomfort, but understandably also wasn't something I could talk about easily.

'How are you, Ellie?'

'Well, aside from a nasty crack in my vajayjay that makes me walk as though I'm smuggling a small newt in my knickers, absolutely tip-top, thanks.'

Hoping a tube of cream would fix the problem, I went to see my GP, a meeting which would spark off years of medical investigations. I've had my vulva poked, prodded and stared at by more doctors than I can care to remember. If you want to know the best angles for posing – talk to my vagine. My lady garden has had more close-ups, and ring lights pointed at it than all of the Hadid sisters combined.

Gynaecologists. Dermatologists. Dermatologists specialising in gynaecology. Gynaecologists specialising in dermatology. Investigations, swabs, biopsies that involved something along the lines of a hole puncher to collect sample sections of skin for analysis. The medical inquiries peaked a few years ago when I ended up being referred to a plastic surgeon. He was trialling a new procedure for women having similar issues to me, many of whom were suffering from a specific chronic skin condition called lichen sclerosus that affects mostly the vulval area and can have a lifelong painful impact on the women it affects. While I had been found not to have lichen sclerosus, I certainly showed many of the same symptoms, so I was booked in for a cutting edge procedure called 'vulval fat transfer'. So far, so L.A. It involved collecting fat cells from my stomach via liposuction (free bit of liposuction on the NHS? Don't mind if I do.) and then injecting those collected cells into the relevant area with the hope they would make it stronger and more sturdy. And, let's be honest, of all the adjectives one can hope to have thrown at our vulvas, 'sturdy' is easily in the top three.

During these investigations, one key conversation always stuck in my mind. It was with the gynaecologist who referred me to the plastic surgeon to get my designer vagina. She said that having problems with the resilience of my skin would mean that if I ever had kids, I might want to think about having a caesarean birth. I took those words, folded them neatly and carried them around in my pocket. Those words were one of the first things I thought about when I found out I was pregnant. If my sister, without a history of volatile skin, ended up with 4th-degree tearing during her first birth, what the hell would I be risking with my already bone china vagina?

At my very first meeting with my midwife, I told her my concerns, and she referred me to a consultant obstetrician.

I'm still not convinced that the meeting I had with that consultant was not some kind of hidden camera sting used to capture a video for teaching hospitals called, 'Arrogance & Superiority: A Physician's Guide to Knobheadery'. In the face of my concern and vulnerability – a pregnant woman for whom even being in a hospital environment was an alien and disarming experience – the consultant was at best, jaded, and at worst, uncaring.

As I told her what the dermatologist had told me a few years previously about considering a C-section, she asked for the doctor's name, whose advice I'd always remembered. I gave the name. The consultant snorted.

'Oh right. Yes . . . I know X . . .', she said mysteriously, laughing to herself. The junior doctor in the room, sitting in the corner 'observing', joined in with the laughter. There was no explanation. 'What the fuck is this?' I thought, 'I'm all for an in-joke, but there's a time and a place, and a conversation where a scared pregnant lady is talking about the survival of her perineum is not one of them.'

I carried on, explaining how I'd only had the fancy fat transfer operation a year previously and that it hadn't really helped too much. I said how I had real fears and anxiety about heading into a vaginal birth, unsure of what extra risks I may be subject to. She dismissed me. She said that if anything, in the long run, perhaps the birth may *help* the skin. Toughen it up. *Toughen it up*. Like she was a Victorian father telling their young son that boarding school, with its daily corporal punishment and a light bit of sadistic buggery, will be the absolute making of him. Yes, it would be an awful, painful, psychologically traumatising ordeal, but at least he'd leave there a man.

I DID NOT WANT MY VAGINA TO BE A MAN.

The consultant refused to grant the C-section, and I left her horrid little kingdom feeling unheard, scared and stupid. But the birth was still a good five months away. I had time to do what I do best. No, not Zumba. *Research.* My first step was to message my GP friend Lyns (the one who I'd shown a picture of my tuppence to in Wagamamas – now you understand why I was so keen to taint her katsu curry experience). She pointed me towards the C-section guidelines published by NICE, the National Institute for Health and Care Excellence, the professional body whose role is to improve outcomes for people using the NHS and other public health services. The guidelines state:

> *'For women requesting a caesarean section, if after discussion and offer of support (including perinatal mental health support for women with anxiety about childbirth), a vaginal birth is still not an acceptable option, offer a planned caesarean section. An obstetrician unwilling to perform a caesarean section should refer the woman to an obstetrician who will carry out the caesarean section.'*

HA. Gotcha, you old witch.

If the evil doctor wouldn't give me a C-section, another doctor would be obliged to. What a golden little nugget. Reading that, combined with a fair amount of reading up on vaginal versus abdominal births, confirmed to me that a C-section was definitely the way I wanted to proceed. Rather ironically, I was going to push for a caesarean.

I went back to my midwife and asked for a referral with a new doctor. She arranged it straight away, and at about seven months pregnant, I found myself back in a hospital room with a new consultant. If the last doctor was the Wicked Witch of the West, then this woman was shining Glinda, complete with stethoscope tiara and hypodermic needle-wand. She listened to me. She heard me. She said that, after hearing my medical history, she could completely understand my reticence in having a vaginal birth. She logged on to her computer, pulled up an online diary and, right then and there, booked me in to have my baby. I've had more trying conversations arranging a cut and blow-dry. She talked me through how it would work, how I had to be at the hospital at 7.00 am, how I wouldn't be able to eat after 12.00 am the night before, so should make sure I have a lovely big dinner washed down with a glass of wine. I thanked her and, as I said my goodbyes, I began to cry. I hadn't realised how much stress had been circling this decision. Knowing that I was now going to have the birth that I felt would be better for my body and mind provided immeasurable relief for me. I rang my husband and asked him what he was doing on the date she'd given me. He said he actually had a physio appointment for that morning but said he'd try and get there in time to catch the end.

As always, with anything related to babies, there will be some women reading this and feeling sad for me because, for them, a C-section would be their worst birth nightmare. Many women passionately want to avoid a caesarean in the same way I passionately wanted to avoid a vaginal birth. I understand that. I adamantly believe every woman should be entitled to the birth they want or need. I would love to say that I was met with support from everyone who heard I had opted for an elective section, but even among friends, that was not the case. I'll always remember having a coffee with a seasoned mother I know who has had four successful vaginal births. When I mentioned I was hoping to secure a caesarean as opposed to going down the veej route, she looked horrified and with a voice filled with confusion, said, 'But don't you want to even *try* it?' like I was turning down a free donut. No, I did not want to *try* 'it'. I didn't want a fun little taster of something that could potentially exacerbate my current problems and leave me with sustained and lifelong damage.

You may have noticed that I use the term 'vaginal birth' rather than 'natural birth'. I think it's an important distinction that I annoyingly try to impose wherever possible. Saying one form of birth is 'natural' by default suggests any other birth is 'unnatural' – a word that I cannot recall ever being used in a positive context. Unnatural. Abnormal. Strange. The glorification of all things 'natural' in childbirth contributes to what seems to be almost a fetishisation of women's suffering during labour. A good birth done 'well' always seems to involve a woman 'enduring'. Many times I have seen a gushing statement on Facebook written by a new father announcing the arrival of a child that involves some glowing praise about his partner that focuses on her 36-hour labour conducted on, '. . . just gas and air. I'm in awe!' as though the lack of pain relief is the achievement rather than the labour or baby. Let me be clear, any woman who starts a day with a child inside her and ends that day holding the child in her arms deserves to be viewed with awe. Whichever way that baby has arrived, that woman has undoubtedly been through the wringer, so let's stop focusing admiration on the amount of pain it is perceived she can bear.

I'm also not saying that opting out of pain relief is not a valid choice for some women, and I can understand why they want to go down that route. I know many women who have ploughed ahead on nothing but their inner warrior and some Strepsils because they wanted to *feel* the whole experience as totally and completely as they can. It is their autonomy, being absolutely immersed in the experience. But at the same time, I wouldn't want any woman to feel she has 'failed' if she changes her mind. As is often said, there are no prizes for childbirth. There is no winners podium with a giant champagne bottle to drench those who just have a couple of paracetamol. The midwives will not pin a picture of you to a board on the ward under a laminated sign saying: 'BIRTH OF THE WEEK!' Neither will you be pelted with faeces on the way to the car park by an angry mob of nurses shouting, 'SHAME! SHAME!', Game of Thrones-style if you end a four-day labour with an emergency C-section. So do whatever you want during the birth. Change your mind. Change it back again. Sometimes someone else will have to decide for you anyway. It's your body, it's your experience, and crucially it's your pain. Not your partner's, not your mum's, not any of the authors whose books you've read. Whether the baby comes out your birth canal or via the sunroof, whether it was what you planned or a complete deviation, whether you have no pain relief and soothe yourself by biting chunks out of your partner's forearm, or you end up off your tits on a euphoric Pethidine high thinking you're labouring a baby giraffe, your birth is your birth. There is no hierarchy. You cannot fail at childbirth. You cannot do it wrong.

8

Farewells

October turned into November, and the entry in my diary that read 'HAVE A BABY' was now in daily view. It may as well have read: '7.00–10.00 am END OF EXISTENCE/ START OF NEW ONE'. There it was, the earmarked day where I'd barter my current reality in exchange for a baby, and the result would be a new way of living I couldn't yet know. This lead-up to my child's birth date was spent undertaking an enjoyably melodramatic process of saying 'adieu' to parts of my life I knew I would never see again, or certainly not for a while.

The earliest pregnancy 'farewell' that I remember was directed at a zip. For some women, their bump doesn't really 'pop' until right at the end of their pregnancy. They're still trotting around in skin-tight Sweaty Betty leggings on their way to barre class well into their third trimester. For me, on the other hand, I did a pregnancy test, immediately felt bloated, changed into a kaftan and ideally would have stayed solely in parachutes for the next nine months. 'Work', however, had other ideas, and when I was around three months pregnant, I found myself attempting to tuck my swollen stomach into a pair of brand new, very unforgiving jeans for a stint of filming. Three long days in those skinny bastards made me impose a strict ban on anything with a rigid waistband for the rest of my pregnancy, and indeed life in general.

A goodbye to my old bras was also on the cards because, just like the universe, my boobs were ever-expanding. Knowing that any bras I bought now would only be a temporary measure led me to discover the most incredible invention of the last 100 years. 'Do you mean WiFi, Ellie? The smallpox vaccine? Vienneta?' No, silly billys – I'm talking about the *bra extender*, a delightful bit of *bonus* bra back strap to hook onto your existing bra allowing you to do nice things like breathe and eat jacket potatoes. However, just as with all great engineering triumphs, the special extender has its physical limitations, and when my old bras started to dig into my torso like an elastic band around an uncooked Cumberland, I admitted defeat and ordered some massive voluminous floppy bralettes. As soon as I plonked my girls into one of these new garments, my bosoms let out an almost audible sigh of relief. 'Well, hello Sloggi crop top,' they exhaled blissfully, before singing Michael Buble's 'Home' in perfect two-part harmony. Farewell, underwire. You can't sit with us.

The next big 'last' to be crossed off the list was 'final holiday as a couple'. Aware our days as a duo were numbered, I declared we must venture on a designated 'babymoon', an Irish driving holiday climaxing with a night in Dublin where we would be seeing American singer and downtown guy, Billy Joel, perform live. It was only when I started telling people where we were headed and why that I realised that not everyone is a Billy Joel fan. Even those who had a solid respect for 'Piano Man' thought travelling to another country to watch BJ in concert as part of mine and Phil's 'final hurrah' was, in the words of my friend Liz, 'Really bloody weird, mate.' I just assumed everyone had a childhood filled with long car journeys to French campsites taking it in turns to spit out the devastating lyrics to 'We Didn't Start the Fire', but apparently not. And, may I say, your loss.

Aside from being the youngest person at the concert by a couple of centuries, my main memory of the babymoon was pissing myself in a yurt. We were glamping in a magical, dreamcatcher-covered tent complete with a king-size bed and views over a quaint harbour town. Ruining this fairytale image somewhat was the puffy, snotty pregnant woman riddled with hay fever, unable to take antihistamines and spluttering all over the vast array of wind chimes that dangled with abundance. During one particularly ferocious sneezing fit, my already strained pelvic floor decided to relinquish responsibility completely, resulting in a puppy-like puddle on the floor. Luckily, the yurt being a yurt, it was windowless and dingy, so I managed to keep the widdle between just me and a hand-woven Mongolian rug, my husband none the wiser. In that moment, I said a double goodbye both to holidays as a carefree married couple and, also, my self-respect.

That babymoon also brought with it another 'last' – 'the final shag'. I have friends who haven't 'done it' for the entirety of their pregnancy, opting out of sex in the same way I periodically unsubscribe from marketing emails from Domino's. I'm not saying I'll never fancy a buy one, get one free 12-inch pepperoni again, but just not right now, cheers. On the flip side, I know some heavily pregnant women who felt very, very sexy. Some of those women happened to be partnered with people who found heavily pregnant women very, very sexy right back. If anyone reading this is in that happily aligned partnership right now, firstly, thanks for taking a break from all that lovely boning, and secondly, may there be many more spectacular (if rather static) sexy sessions ahead of you before your child arrives.

In my case, as my pregnancy progressed, I simply got to a point where sex seemed *silly*. It wasn't that I suddenly hated the idea of it, more that, when I saw myself in a mirror, my new physicality just screamed 'clown'. And clowns aren't sexy. Scary, sure, enigmatic, absolutely – but sexy? No way *honks red nose to underline point*. I just looked so *funny*. There was my bump, a solid obtrusive boulder. There were my legs, 50% cellulite, 50% lemon drizzle cake. There were my giant, veiny boobies topped with nipples that had morphed from small transparent 10p pieces to big dark blobs the size and colour of chocolate digestives. I grunted when I moved. I had many new chin friends. I was never more than one metre away from my pillow-in-a-bag. I looked and felt absurd. Not bad, not yucky, just *funny* – I was a walking punchline. I was the physical incarnation of a person slipping on a banana skin. My reaction, after the last time we 'did it' while pregnant, was similar to the thoughts I experience every Boxing Day morning when I find myself sitting in front of my parent's fridge spooning leftover trifle directly into my mouth with a serving spoon – 'Probably enough for now.'

Then there was my baby shower, otherwise known as: 'the last time I will be the centre of attention'. Often, nowadays, a pregnant woman's final girl group meet up will be at her shower, even if it's something low-key involving just a few women having dinner and discussing the mother-to-be's hopes, plans and childbirth fears (the latter usually involving something about induction and/or shitting during labour. It's always about shitting during labour). Or perhaps the baby shower will be a bigger affair – a raucous day in a hot pub function room where 25 women take it in turns to sniff nappies filled with 'poo' made from melted chocolate bars, and say things like, 'Hmm, this one's grainy . . . I reckon Toffee Crisp. Write it on the whiteboard, Sue!' I've been to both kind of shower and have to say that for me, any event that doesn't involve someone microwaving a Yorkie to wipe in the gusset of a Pampers is my preferred way to spend a few hours.

My own baby shower was an afternoon tea in a trendy hotel where all my favourite women came to wish me bon voyage as I set sail aboard HMS *Leaky Tits*. There I sat, scoffing scones, laden with my big round belly, watching friends from every stage of my life chat and laugh, and asking my mum if she wanted another crustless ham sandwich that was going spare (she did). As I thanked each of these women for their thoughtful gifts and their beautiful cards filled with wonderful sentiments, I remember thinking back to Ellie, aged 25, who maintained that baby showers were frivolous, greedy and, worst of all, *American*.

A decade on, my cynicism has been replaced with a deep affection. Baby showers are now my favourite type of 'event'. Screw birthday parties or weddings – too much hanging around and Spanx-wearing. Baby showers, on the other hand, are understated, incredibly personal and best of all, *a little bit witchy*. Perhaps that's why I like them so much – because I've come to see them as less of an event and more of a ritual. A ritual where at an agreed date and time, a group of women congregate with the sole aim of cherishing a fellow sister, ensuring her extraordinary transition into 'Mother' begins with her being coated, soaked, *sodden* in love. As I left my shower, my heart bursting with female connection, holding gift bags bursting with tiny outfits and eleven identical Sophie the Giraffes, I thought to myself how lucky I was to be surrounded by such a lovely bunch of witches. There'd been no cauldron, no ceremony, just slabs of Genoise sponge and gift boxes of Infacol, but there'd been magic there, in that room.

And then, before I knew it, I was saying goodbye to the final few 'lasts', knowing that the next time I'd be doing these things would be as a parent. There was the 'last work event' – a gig in Liverpool when I was two weeks away from giving birth, where the promoter jokingly pointed out a mop and bucket in the wings 'just in case'. Then came my 'last solo walk'. An autumn evening, the sun setting as I sobbed my way round the park, listening to the Broadway cast recording of *Waitress The Musical* where the pregnant main character sings moving ballads to both her younger self and her unborn baby. So much bloody pathos.

The days whistled by, and, before long, it was the 'last day of being childfree.' Phil took the day off work, and we had a lazy morning of the 'last tea and toast while watching *Frasier*', followed by the 'last trip to the cinema'. I'd chosen to see one of the *Harry Potter* spin-off movies, and, as I settled into the chair (involving the 'last official engagement of my pillow-in-a-bag') the lights went down, and so began one of the dullest films ever made. After 30 minutes, I decided that, as much as I enjoy hearing Eddie Redmayne's voice (which I always think sounds like he's mid-burp), this was a waste of my consciousness. I instead opted for a tactical sleep. Rumour has it that babies can be *quite* tiring, so I reasoned that if I had the opportunity to squeeze in a 'last nap before you have a dependant' then I should. I powered down like a robot. The film ended. I powered up, brushed the popcorn off my bump and trekked home for a takeaway Nando's, which I managed to shovel in despite a fair amount of snivelling. Phil sat next to me on the sofa, enveloped me in a huge cuddle and asked why I was crying. What I meant to say was: 'Because tomorrow is the biggest day of our lives. Because I'm worried about the change to everything we've ever known. Because I'm worried about my own safety having this huge operation. Because it's all too vast to have laid out in front of me while I'm just eating a chicken pitta like everything is normal and it isn't.' What I actually said was punctuated by snot bubbles and sounded something like, 'Wahhhwahhh baby wahhh'. Phil stayed next to me, and my whimpering slowed. We watched some *Modern Family*, I had the glass of wine my consultant had suggested, nay, *ordered* me to have, and then we went to bed, knowing that this was to be the 'last night of sleep'. I stared at the ceiling. Seeing as I find it hard to drift off on the evening before a *Great British Bake Off* final due to excitement, there was never much chance of a brilliant night's sleep the night before having a human cut out of me. I picked up my phone. Cue the 'last time I'll enter an Instagram scroll hole and find myself 2016-deep into Patsy Palmer's account'. Eventually, though, Patsy worked her magic (she's doing very well in LA, FYI), and as sleep began to creep up on me, I put down my phone, heaved myself onto my side and whispered my last goodnight to the bump.

9

Birth

There is no hiding the fact that giving birth is still, even today, a potentially risky biological business for both mother and baby. Carrying and then evacuating a child either vaginally or abdominally poses multiple potential issues, the majority of which can now, fortunately, be navigated by our advanced medical knowledge and incredible health service. Women giving birth in the UK today face considerably brighter odds compared even to our grandmothers. In the 1950s, when my Nanny Cook gave birth to my mum, it was estimated 69 women died for every 100,000 live births in England and Wales. When I gave birth to Nanny Cook's great-granddaughter that figure had fallen to nine. It goes without saying that nine women dying is still nine women too many, but when compared to the numbers in Sierra Leone – which sadly has the highest maternal mortality ratio in the world at 1,360 per 100,000 live births – it seems that Britons feeling 'lucky' to have the NHS is a gross understatement. On the face of it, then, the UK is smashing maternal healthcare. Embarrassingly, though, that's not entirely true.

Just a few years ago, the UK, one of the world's wealthiest countries, only just scraped into the top 25 of Save the Children's State of the World's Mothers report – coming in at number 24 and trailing behind the likes of Slovenia and Luxembourg. Then, more recently, Oxford University released a shocking report on UK maternity care that found: '*a five-fold difference in maternal mortality rates amongst women from Black ethnic backgrounds and an almost two-fold difference amongst women from Asian ethnic backgrounds compared to white women*'.[1] Simply put, an Asian woman is twice as likely to die when carrying her child, giving birth to her child or during her postpartum period than a white woman and for black women that rises to *five times as likely*. I defy anyone reading those facts for the first time not to be left open-mouthed. Or perhaps I should say I defy any *white* people reading those facts for the first time not to be left open-mouthed. I suspect that for British women of colour, while the stats may be unbelievably alarming, the revelation itself that yet another part of the system isn't protecting them equally comes as little surprise. While it's true that in the grand scheme of world health, every woman who has their baby in the UK is comparatively lucky, this report shows an ugly truth – that you're luckier if you're white. That is intolerable. It's a systemic failing Britain needs to fix urgently. I know I can't do justice to this issue and the experiences of women impacted by it. For that, Candice Brathwaite's extraordinary book *I Am Not Your Baby Mother* is essential reading.

My point here is not to scare any pregnant women into running for the hills, taking refuge in a barn and giving birth behind a tractor like a stray cat, but rather to reiterate that

1 Knight M, Bunch K, Tuffnell D, Shakespeare J, Kotnis R, Kenyon S, Kurinczuk JJ (Eds.) on behalf of MBRRACE-UK. Saving Lives, Improving Mothers' Care - Lessons learned to inform maternity care from the UK and Ireland Confidential Enquiries into Maternal Deaths and Morbidity 2015-17. Oxford: National Perinatal Epidemiology Unit, University of Oxford 2019.

having a baby is a big bloody deal and, even in the UK, can sometimes be accompanied with risks. It often seems, however, that those inherent risks are forgotten or simply deemed unworthy of acknowledgement, as though diluted by the sheer frequency that birth occurs. Society's attitude to women giving birth is similar to my attitude to someone doing a 5k fun run in a sequinned bra. *Oh, for god's sake, what's all the fuss about? OK, yes, it'll be a bit tough at points, but you're not the first to do it, Louise, and you won't be the last, so once it's over and you've got the medal, there's really no need to talk about it again. And no, I will absolutely not sponsor you.*

Each day in the UK, around 2000 new little humans are pushed, pulled and plucked into their first day on this planet – an occurrence so commonplace, so run of the mill, that the inherent jeopardy circling each one of those births is easily disregarded. And yet, *every* birth is a seismic event. Every single birth, every single day, creates a new gravitational pull in that woman's universe. And so it was for me as my alarm went off on the morning of my C-section. I reached for Phil's hand and gripped it tightly under the covers, swallowing down thoughts of events unfolding in a way that would be anything other than absolutely fine. It's a rare thing in life to open your eyes on one day, knowing that when you close them again that night, your life will be brand new.

We were due at the hospital at 7.00 am. I had decided that instead of lapping up every final minute of the 'last morning doze in a warm careless bed', I should instead set my alarm for 5.00 am, so I would have time to curl my hair. It seemed while my very essence knew that the next 24 hours were to be unimaginably profound, a very unprofound part of me was viewing the whole event through the prism of it being 'a selfie-heavy day'. That same part of me was also responsible for including a hairdryer and GHD straighteners in my hospital bag, because we all know how newborn babies bond better with mothers who have volume and bounce. Another questionable addition to my packing, along with the standard baby clothes and nappies, was a notepad and pen – there, just in case, while recovering from abdominal surgery, trying to ride an out of control hormonal bucking bronco and coming to terms with the magnitude of motherhood, I had any super kool creative ideas I wanted to jot down. Perhaps a jaunty sitcom top line about a grandma and grandson detective duo, for instance, or maybe a haiku inspired by the hospital's catering. Needless to say, I clearly had an extremely accurate understanding of life with a newborn, and those NCT classes had been worth every penny.

In a strange turn of events, when I'd finally let go of Phil's sleeping hand and trundled to the bathroom (the 'last getting out of bed to tend only to myself and no one else'), my morning Gusspection™ (yes, it's still in use) was met with the sight of what could only be Janet's bloody oyster. Well, what are the bloody chances! Clearly, my child knew it was her designated eviction day and had decided to get things moving of her own accord. While I thought that my 'show' was a charming coincidence (I imagine this is the only time the expulsion of a mucus plug has been called charming) I also started to experience a dull ache in my stomach which was not so beguiling. As idiotic as it seems now, it took me a while to realise that the strange pains that forced me to periodically down tools (hair tongs) were actually contractions.

Not being car owners and the hospital being only ten minutes away, we'd always planned to walk there (the 'last stroll as a duo'), so at 6.45 am we left the house (the 'last time locking the Chubb while childfree'). We wandered slowly through the black winter morning, smiling at some early rising neighbours through their kitchen windows. They knew exactly what this sight meant, their cheerful waves turning them into pyjama-clad guards of honour lining the route. Phil lingered next to me, carrying my bags and acting as official wildlife photographer, capturing the all-important video of The Giant Pregnant Lady, who had begun breathing heavily and occasionally stopping to lean against a wall as another rush of pain surged. It had begun to take my breath away. It felt urgent and wild, as though my own body was beginning to crush me from within. Needless to say, this was not part of the plan. Sure, it would be a lovely twist of events in a TV show (I made a mental note to scribble it down in my notebook as soon as I could see again), a lady due to have a planned C-section splashing down her baby in the Co-op en route to the labour ward, but in real life, I hadn't written these contractions into the pre-scripted narrative of my birth, and they needed to stop. Immediately.

I must have experienced about two hours of this pain in total, and I assume that the contractions I had were just the fringes of what full labour involves. As such, I can categorically state that, much like Aperol Spritz, vaginal birth is not for me. To all the billions of women who have done it the vajayjay way, I humbly bow down at your feet (and vulvas).

Once at the hospital, we were taken to a cubicle, and I swiftly received some drugs to delay the progression of what was going on naturally. Thankfully, the medication kicked in quickly and I began to think clearly again just in time to be faced with a nurse asking if I was wearing any make-up.

'You aren't allowed make-up in theatre,' she said. 'The anaesthetist needs to be able to see your true skin colour,' her eyes flicking to my clearly mascaraed lashes framed by some niftily contoured temples. I looked back blankly.

'No problem,' I said, 'I'm only wearing moisturiser.' We stared at one another. Silence.

After a few agonising seconds, the stand-off ended, as she handed me some surgical stockings and disappeared through the curtains. Success – either my Jedi mind trick had worked or, more likely, she was too busy to argue with a woman clearly covered in at least three coats of Benefit Hoola bronzer. In my defence, I'd done everything else that had been asked of me. I'd taken off all my nail varnish (another stipulation before operations in order for the colour of your nail beds to be clearly seen), I'd eaten nothing since my sobby Nando's the night before, I'd swallowed the pre-op pills I'd been given and I'd even waxed my own bush in order to create a neat work surface for the surgeon (no easy feat when you can't get a direct eye line to the place in question, meaning you have to rely on a strategically placed hand mirror and a lot of faith). I have a huge respect for medical professionals. I value their guidance, their dedication and will happily give them a big old clap whenever social media tells me to, but it's crucial to remember, and I cannot overemphasise this, that as previously stated this was going to be an *incredibly selfie-heavy day*. I had done a risk assessment and decided that, quite simply, some things are more important than a doctor seeing if you're turning blue, and those things are photos of yourself with the tanned dewy cheeks of a young J Lo (the Affleck years).

And obviously, I had done my research. I'd consulted my

v. good friend The Internet about wearing slap during an elective C-section (ELCS), and a quick search had revealed multiple forum threads on this hot subject because, well, of course there were. There are forums on every subject you can imagine. Somewhere online right now, people will be arguing on a forum about the pros and cons of forums. Now, on this particular forum, entitled something like, 'ELCS - foundation?', there were two groups of women. The first were people like me who wanted to begin motherhood looking like 'themselves' both in real life and, more importantly, on the 'gram, versus a second opposing group who labelled even *thinking* about make-up while having baby, vain, unnecessary and ideally ending in a custodial sentence. This group posted lots of things along the lines of, 'Err, it's surgery, not a fashion show,' spiralling into the more dramatic, 'Get over yourself! I have twin boys – the closest I've come to self-care since they were born is pretending the Weetabix they lob at my head is Crème de la Mer face cream. ABANDON ALL HOPE.'

Now, I can understand why a woman undertaking a *vaginal* birth wouldn't see the benefit of applying a precise black flick before heading into an arduous physical labour that could last days. That eyeliner will be all over the shop before you can say, 'Claudia Winkleman with conjunctivitis'. And yet, I know some women who did just that. I have a few friends who popped on a bit of concealer and a sweep of powder before their labours really ramped up so they could at least start the process feeling like themselves, because by the end of it, they had no idea who they would be. As with everything in regard to birth and babies, do whatever you want, mate. Get a spray tan, don't get a spray tan. Stick on fake lashes, stick to just lip balm. Veet everything, Veet nothing. Choose life.

While I changed into a robe and compression socks the length of the M1, Phil put on the scrubs he'd been given and, like every single man who'd gone before him, decided he looked incredible and should immediately retrain to be George Clooney from 1997. An hour or so of sitting in the cubicle whispering giddy nonsense and inappropriate jokes about the fact I didn't have any knickers on, we were told it was time. Guided by a midwife, we headed down to the operating theatre, Phil's hands both full; my jittery paw in one, and a bag of tiny clothes for our daughter in the other.

We walked into the theatre, both crowned with silly hairnets that made us look like we'd just finished a shift on the cheese counter. The room was full of medical staff (a good start) who welcomed us warmly. A nurse pointed to the bed in the middle of the theatre and asked me to 'pop' myself on the edge. Nothing dilutes a direction to climb onto an operating table where you will soon be sliced open, better than a cheerful deployment of the word 'pop'. It was like Phil 'popping' the question with a proposal all over again, but this time, I appreciated the honeyed language. Anything to de-escalate the weirdness of the situation was welcome.

The anaesthetist explained that he was now going to administer my spinal block, which would numb me from the chest down. Perching on the bed, I hunched forward, rounding my body and offered my back towards the needle I hadn't wanted to look at. The nice nurse sat in front of me, patting my knee and telling me how brave I was as tears of pain and concern and a million other feelings fell onto my gown. Christ, this was really happening. The anaesthetist finished, the nurse dabbed away my tears with a tissue, congratulating me on getting the 'nasty bit' over with. 'She is so kind,' I thought,

'They are all *so* kind.' (There was also a small part of me that thought, 'Oh for god's sake, she's probably wiped off all my Touche Éclat. Doesn't she know it's going to be a selfie-heavy day?' But we'll park that there.)

I laid down on the table, and everyone introduced themselves, saying their name and their job title, like a medical episode of *Blind Date*. It seems odd now to think that I can't remember any of those people. I couldn't recall their names if you paid me a million pounds, their identities wiped away by the adrenalin surging inside me so focused on myself and my child. But, in a perfectly cliched way, while I don't remember any specifics about them, I remember how they made me feel. Throughout the whole experience, the atmosphere in the theatre was so *joyful*, and that will always be the word I use to describe my daughter's birth. I am incredibly grateful for that. She was lifted into joy.

As they got to work erecting a screen under my neck to obscure the business end, Phil fired up a small Bluetooth speaker and the playlist he'd made for the occasion (entitled 'D Day' – I'm listening to it as I write this chapter) began belting out. Stevie Wonder's 'You Are the Sunshine of My Life' filled the room, the team got going with their preparations, a dance in their step, occasionally singing along to music while checking in on me.

There was one slightly unusual moment where one of the team popped his head over my little neck curtain and said he'd very much enjoyed my *Live at the Apollo* performance, which is the first (and hopefully last time) I've been recognised while being catheterised. (The anaesthetist, sitting right next to me for the whole procedure, then made a point of re-assuring me that everything that happens in hospital is, of course, completely confidential, which was his way of saying, 'Sorry about that – I promise he won't inform *Grazia* about your unevenly waxed bonnet.')

As the anaesthetic kicked in, the surgeon announced he was about to start the operation. I gripped Phil's hand – my own shaking uncontrollably by now (a common side effect of the drugs), a little concerned that the spinal block hadn't worked properly because, as they got stuck in, I could sense movement like a rough pulling and pushing.

And then we heard a bleat. Phil and I stared at each other, two grinning shower-capped loons. The cry became a wail, and then there she was, the little mystery inside me finally revealed, being held above the curtain, bloody and angry, limbs rigid, furious to have been dragged from her dark cosy den into this stark world. She was scrawny and squashed, and had a head shape that reminded me of Homer Simpson's dad. Off she went out of my line of sight to be weighed under the watchful eye of her daddy and his GoPro, who followed after. All I could do was lie there, staring at the ceiling, smiling and chuckling to myself, happy tears running into my curled hair and ruining my contoured temples en route. She was here. Finally, she was here, and then she was being laid under my chin, this funny little creature, now quiet and wide-eyed. As I held my daughter for the first time, telling her how nice it was to meet her and that my name was Mummy, I realised that Mariah Carey's 'All I Want for Christmas is You' was tinkling out of the theatre speakers. Phil, knowing that it's one of my favourite songs (and one that featured at our wedding), had secretly added it to the birth playlist. It was perfect. Sunny, camp and, bearing in mind it was still November, utterly ridiculous. That song means even more to me now. My poor Ratbag gets hurled round the room every time it plays on the radio during the festive period. I imagine she counts down the days until January 1st when she can start her annual whiplash convalescence.

I lay there in theatre for a little longer, locked in a stare-off with my quiet child as the surgeons bustled around, saying things we didn't understand – including the memorable line: 'Time to clean the gutters'. To this day, I have no idea what gutters are, but I take solace in the fact at least mine have been cleaned. Once all my insides had been tucked back in and glued shut, we moved into the recovery area, Phil and I thanking every one of the operating team annoyingly earnestly as we left as a little family. Before long, I was sitting up in bed and my baby girl, wrapped in a warmed towel fresh from a linen cupboard, was on my boob, seeking a bit of refreshment after a rather trying morning.

It's all a little hazy after that. I remember being wheeled back to the ward where we'd started the day, and our baby sleeping quietly in a little cot next to me, still wrapped in a towel as none of the outfits we'd bought fitted her. We were told she was going to be a 10lb whopper, but she'd come out at 7lb 8 ounces and needed smaller clothes. She was skinny, and her lanky legs remained firmly tucked close to her sides making her look like a little frozen chicken. We couldn't physically get her into the massive babygros we'd bought and, in the end, called in an emergency delivery of newborn sleepsuits which we then cut the feet out of in order to manoeuvre the strange little leggy creature inside.

I remember Phil fetching me a croque monsieur from the hospital's café and it being unbelievably average, and then him having to leave because of the strict visiting hours the ward kept. High on drugs and hormones, I'm pretty sure I spent that solo time WhatsApping photos of me with my new baby girl (and my great hair) to anyone I'd ever met, as opposed to doing what I should have been doing, which was, of course, sleeping. I remember Phil returning and asking a midwife if it was normal that the baby was so quiet and sleepy, and should we wake her up. The midwife laughed kindly and said we should make the most of it. I imagine what she was actually thinking was, 'PAHAHAHAHAHA! What a pair of chumps!' My parents and sister came to visit. More photos of my child and hair were taken, and as afternoon fell and darkness licked at the windows, a side room became available, and a nurse asked if I would like it. I said I would, very much. She said that, seeing as it was time for me to try and stand up anyway, we may as well combine the two things. If I wanted the room, I was going to have to walk there.

This moment was a line in the sand. There was the 'before', where I was rejoicing smugly about my perfect day and perfect birth and how well my blusher had stayed on. And then I was attempting to swing my feet off the bed and came face to face with my 'after', which turned out to be a lovely bit of unbridled agony. Smacked with a pain so ferocious and all-consuming, I assumed something had gone terribly wrong. This couldn't be right. Phil, trying to be supportive, reasoned that, 'Maybe the surgeon left something inside you'. I thought afterwards how I should have said something along the lines of, 'I wish I'd never let *you* inside me', but it turns out that abject torment puts pay to quick comebacks.

I had expected my recovery to be painful, but this sheer torment hadn't been on my radar at all. My sister had had an ELCS with her second baby, and she'd raved about it. She was strolling around the ward within hours, she said, sure a bit sore but nothing too major in the grand scheme of things. Buoyed by her experience, I'd gone on to read multiple other accounts on pregnancy forums (yes, more forums) about how healing from a caesarean really wasn't that bad. Of course, there'd be the occasional post to the contrary, along the lines of, 'Holy mackerel, you girls were so lucky! I found my C-section recuperation horrific!' Reading through the exchanges, I thought to myself how pleased I was that Holy Mackerel Lady was clearly in the minority, and how fortunate it was that I was so unlikely to share her experience. And yet, surprise! *Je Suis* Holy Mackerel Lady.

The most minuscule adjustment of my leg made my abdomen feel like it was bursting open, so much so, I insisted a nurse check my wound. I was convinced that – at any moment – one of my stomach muscles would flop out onto the sheets, and I would be able to say, 'See! What did the surgeon glue me up with? Pritt Stick?!' The nurse lifted my gown and reassured me that everything looked absolutely fine. I couldn't believe it. I tried again to inch my way off the bed, hoping it was just an initial problem. Perhaps now I was 'warmed up' I'd be cha-cha-sliding across the floor in no time. No such luck. The agony clawed at me, and I screamed like a frightened child. Millimetre by millimetre, I attempted to edge forward, every minuscule shift in my position ripping through my body, the whole time yelling out as this all-con-suming physical anguish swallowed me up.

I asked Phil to leave the cubicle. It was a strange animalistic instinct – this vulnerability was mortifying. The nurse patiently stayed with me, holding my hands and encouraging me on. The noises that came out of my mouth were the most primal thing I had ever made or heard. Wails of torment with tears streaming down my face. Phil later said that the sounds he heard while outside the drawn curtain were like something you'd hear in an off-radar interrogation facility.

After perhaps 30 minutes of stop-starting, I made it to a hunched standing position and then eventually to a nearby chair where the nurse helped me into a nightie and changed my enormous sodden maternity pad, so soaked with blood it had swollen to the approximate size of a Renault Espace. I was ashamed of this feebleness. I was pathetic. It was around this point that I started to think that if I ever heard anyone again suggest that caesareans are an easy way out, then I would, without hesitation, be forced to scoop their eyes from their sockets like dregs of food caught in the kitchen plughole. That thought gave me the fuel I needed to eventually shuffle over, one agonising step at a time, to the side room. The journey must have been about 10 metres, and I used my catheter stand as a little wheelie walking stick the whole way, but I did it! I'd scaled my Everest! Me and my trusty catheter! Best buds, and what a team! As long as I could always pee into a bag and didn't have to move at all, in any way, ever again, this would all be absolutely doable. Now I thought about it, it was obvious. All I needed to do was lie in this quiet little room until the baby was one or two years old, and I would never have to experience the agony of motion again. Simple! What an interesting childhood my daughter would have, living on vending machine Quavers and learning how to insert cannulas. I was so glad I'd worked out such a reasonable plan.

As Phil unpacked my things, I asked for more Oramorph (a liquid derivative of morphine) that I knocked back like tequila. I couldn't work out if it was helping the pain, exactly, but it definitely made me feel drunk, which seemed like a good place to start. The relief of surviving the walk to the room and no longer being in the grips of violent pain led to a dizzy elation that showed itself via a rambling monologue about how sensational the pack of Jaffa Cakes were that I was busy scoffing. I was exhilarated. Not only did I have a baby, I also had a WHOLE PACKET OF BISCUITS! Life was wild! How fun and tasty motherhood was turning out to be!

A nurse came in and said it was time to remove my catheter. Crap. My foolproof plan to never move again was under attack. I pleaded to keep it in. I explained how moving caused me exceptional pain, and there was no way I would be able to make it to a toilet without, I assumed, dying. I lowered my voice conspiratorially and told her that if she left the catheter in, I'd *consider* giving her a Jaffa. She declined. So out came my cherished wee hose, and instead, I was presented with a plastic jug that looked like something you'd make Bisto gravy in. The midwife told me that when I next needed to pee, I was to do it straight into the transparent jug so a nurse could have a lovely look at my urine. Would the indignity never end? (No. No, it wouldn't).

As night set in, we decided that rather than Phil attempting to sleep in the chair in the corner of the room, he would go home to our bed for some proper rest, leaving me and the babe to have our first sleepover. So, with a kiss goodbye for both his girls and a quick check to make sure I had all the essentials within arm's reach (water bottle, phone, Jaffas), he left. And there we were, just me and my daughter. I settled in for one of the strangest nights of my life, peaking in the early hours when I could no longer defy the strain of my bladder I'd been desperately ignoring. Movement remained my sworn enemy, but I had no other option. At least I had an electric bed that could help me get into a seated position. Trying not to disturb the sleeping baby, I internalised my shrieks of torment as I painstakingly manoeuvred myself into a hunched T-Rex stance, took the gravy jug and shuffled myself out of the room and onto the ward outside. I realised at this point that I didn't know what I was meant to do with the baby.

It felt a bit like being in a café, braving a trip to the counter to order another coffee and leaving your laptop on the table unsupervised. What if someone stole my baby before I'd had the chance to back her up to the Cloud? I considered trying to take her with me, perhaps using my teeth to grip onto her sleepsuit as I hovered over the loo and weed into the jug, but then remembered that my daughter was a human and not a handbag I didn't want to put on the floor of a nightclub toilet. I decided she was probably fine where she was, so continued to the bathroom, where it took a mere ten hours to pull down my giant knickers before wedging the jug between my thighs and doing the biggest wee of my life. I don't know if it was fluid retention or if, perhaps, the baby had been lying on my intestines for so long inside me I'd forgotten what it was like to have a bladder at full capacity, but this was the whizz to end all whizzes, and let me tell you, I enjoyed every moment.

Once Niagara had run dry, I staggered out of the bathroom and began a search for a nurse to check all was OK with my offering. I don't know if you've ever roamed a dark hospital floor in the middle of the night while holding a giant receptacle of your own steaming urine with the sole aim of making a stranger stare at it, but it certainly made my list of top three 'Memorable Errands'. Eventually, I found a nurse to do the wee observation. She said it all looked fine, and rewarded me for my efforts with another shot of Oramorph. I lumbered back to my room, still holding the precariously full pee pee jug, to find that my child was still there. Phew. I got back in bed and heaved the now stirring baby onto my chest, where she remained for the rest of the night. I stared at her funny little face in the low light, both of us slipping in and out of sleep.

Morning came, and my husband arrived at the hospital with some specific supplies I had made him source ('Apple juice. It must be expensive and cloudy. And a sausage sandwich but not the fancy sort. I want a basic, dirty sausage. 100% pure eyelid and bumhole.') As he opened the door to my room, the first thing I apparently said as I lay there feeding our daughter was, 'Phil . . . I really like her.'

After spending the day having various checks and tests in the late afternoon, a doctor came to discharge us. I asked him about the pain medication he would be sending me home with. The answer, which I still find incredulous, turned out to be a big fat nothing. There I was, having just had major abdominal surgery, multiple layers of skin, flesh and muscle needing to heal and bond back together, and yet the (male) doctor was explaining that he would be writing no prescription. He said any drugs to ease my suffering would be inadvisable because the medication in question could pass through my milk into my child, and, in fact, the same was true about the Oramorph I'd been knocking back with glee for the last 12 hours. To new naive parents, this sounded terrifying. I'd been poisoning my own baby! BURN THE WITCH. In our vulnerability, we accepted his assessment. It seemed that even though the tiniest readjustment of my body remained (and I say this without exaggeration) sheer agony, petrol station paracetamol and ibuprofen were my only 'responsible' options.

Looking back on this exchange now, I refuse to believe that a man's pain would be disregarded in this way. Can you honestly, imagine a man being sawn in half, a human removed, stitched back up and then shoved out the door less than 24 hours later with nothing more than a packet of fucking Nurofen? There it is again, the belief that a 'good' woman and, especially, a 'good' mother is one that must endure. She must stay in pain for the sake of the child, with no consideration that a mother who cannot breathe without wincing, cough without crying or move without cursing may not, in fact, be the best mother right now.

While, of course, the effect on the baby via breast milk is a vital consideration, surely the child should not be the *only* consideration. As with all things, the risks and benefits must be weighed up as a whole. It is not a mother's duty to throw herself under a pain-bus for the child. Birth involves two people. The mother's wellbeing is as important as the child's. It is not enough for a woman to merely 'survive'; whatever her birth experience and recovery may be – survival should be the very minimum. Instead, let's aspire for all women to have the *best* birth and recovery possible and to not just 'get through it and get home', forced to internalise their trauma and pain. Let's aim for more. Let's support women from pregnancy into the post-partum period in a way that puts them front and centre, and not barged out the way, ignored by an overwhelmed system too busy hurrying the queue along and shouting out: 'NEXT!'.

I've spoken to other women who've had C-sections (both

emergency and planned) who share my experience – being sent home with nothing more than paracetamol. Some who were guilted off medication due to concerns about breast-feeding, and others who were formula feeding and still received nothing. I've been contacted by midwives and obstetricians who are appalled by the advice I was given and who have stated that, in their opinion, sending a woman home after abdominal surgery with over-the-counter medicine you'd take for a hangover is not OK. I've also heard from other mothers who instead received everything their druggy heart desired. One in four pregnant women in the UK has a caesarean, so where is the consistency? Why is each individual woman seemingly at the mercy of their individual doctor's views? I naively thought that what had happened to me happened to everyone who'd had an ELCS. That it was NHS policy. And why wouldn't I? A qualified doctor stood in front of an igno-ramus (me) and essentially said that a good mother would suck up any discomfort for the sake of her child. Why would I think any different? How would I know that in the depths of my weakness, I could not rely on this medical professional to care for me and should, in fact, advocate for my own wellbeing? In the end, once I was home after an agonising few days not knowing how I could possibly cope any longer, I called my friend Lyns for advice. As a GP herself, Lyns told me to ring my own doctor immediately and explain the situ-ation. I did and was prescribed something stronger straight away. There were options all along. And yet, the hospital doctor seemed to hide them from me.

Writing this chapter, along with speaking to other women who have shared similar stories to mine (and also women who received no extra pain relief after episiotomies, considerable tearing or injuries from forceps deliveries) has made me see that what I experienced is not just something 'uncool' to bitch about with friends but, in fact, a more important issue regarding, in my opinion, sub-standard care. Since revisiting it, I decided to request a birth review from my hospital. I wanted to know why the beginning of my parenting experience was tarnished. My request resulted in a call with a sympathetic senior member of the maternity unit staff who did their best to explain the reasons for what happened, essentially saying if I'd have made it clearer that I was in real discomfort at the time, I *could* have been discharged with better pain relief. I responded by saying that in my opinion it should never be the responsibility of a new bleeding mother to negotiate for medication. While I can't say I left the conversation reassured that other women at their most vulnerable wouldn't end up in the same position I had found myself in, I appreciated the chance to explain my experience, and if nothing else, have learnt the hard way how vital it is to speak boldly in hospital scenarios. Ultimately, I will always resent that doctor who sent me home. I hope one day, very soon, he falls off his adult scooter (he looked the adult scooter sort), twists an ankle and, when he asks for pain relief, all he is offered is a Canesten pessary.

Respect.
Women's.
Pain.

Once the poopbag doctor left the room, Phil began bustling around packing up my belongings. I stared at my suitcase lying open on the floor, flaunting my stupidity. Hello GHDs. Hiya hairdryer. Hey, notebook and pen. Sorry lads – bit of a pointless trip for you. Under them was also the brand new 'going home' outfit I would never wear with the zip-up boots I would be unable to bend down and put on for weeks. The hospital departure I'd imagined, involved freshly coiffed hair, a new dress toning beautifully with my ruby red Doc Martens and a farewell laugh with the midwives as I read them a sonnet I'd penned in my little Moleskine. The hospital departure I ending up having involved a wheelchair, a coat draped over my stained nightie like a nana escaping a nursing home, my feet in slippers, Mum pushing me along endless corridors and the lights flickering as my husband followed behind, holding the car seat now full with our sleeping, slightly jaundiced little frozen chicken.

As we made our way outside to my parents' car, the fresh winter night hit my bare legs like a slap. With my mum and Phil guiding me, I tearfully made it into the front seat, and, with my dad driving, we began our journey home, every speed bump a fresh mini-agony. And then Phil was carrying our new flatmate into the house, Mum and Dad were kissing me goodbye, and there she was, on the living room floor, asleep in her seat. I examined her from an armchair, trying to work out what on Earth happened now. Twenty-four hours ago, I'd been in the middle of my ode to Jaffa Cakes, full of light and laughter. Where was my light now? Was it still in that side room, pissed out into the jug I'd left on the windowsill, perhaps? Or maybe it was lurking at the bottom of the final shot of Oramorph I'd felt I had to refuse for the sake of my daughter. Sitting there, the house felt strange. And I felt stranger.

10

Newborn

Everyone has a very different post-birth experience; for some, the newborn bubble is the happiest time of their lives, as they find themselves blissfully head over heels in smoochie adoration for their new small housemate. For others, it may not be 24/7 sheer elation, but it is certainly something they have found manageable and enjoyable. Then there are people like me, who find the whole thing, how can I put . . . extremely challenging. I would be doing a disservice to myself, mothers in general and you, my very attractive reader, if I wasn't honest, so I'll openly say that the newborn days were some of the hardest months of my life. To misquote Charles Dickens, 'It was the worst of times, it was the worst of times.' But before I get into all that sunny stuff, I must also say that I would be doing you *another* disservice if I didn't state (and italicise in uppercase) that while my sadness and regret was, at the time, real and all-consuming, it was also transitory. *TRANSITORY*.

If you are reading this while considering having a child, or you're a pregnant woman now trembling in her maternity leggings, or maybe a new mum smack bang in the middle of this and can't see a way through, then please remember that all the uncomfortable things I describe – the thoughts, the feelings, the pain – passed. All of them. Even the piles.

My account of early motherhood is only one of my truths. It's a truth from the past that bears no resemblance to how I feel today. As I write this, I can hear my obnoxiously cute daughter in the kitchen pretending to talk on her 'phone', which is actually a pack of chipolatas she's taken to liberating from the freezer. Now the years have passed, my joyful vantage point feels so far removed from those early days; looking back is like trying to recall a plot from a play I fell asleep watching many moons ago.

There is a wonderful children's book by Michael Rosen called, *We're Going on a Bear Hunt*, that I read – hell, who am I kidding – *performed* for my girl. It's a charming tale of a family going on a stroll with the sole aim, we can only assume, being the premeditated slaying of a bear. Putting their murderous intentions to one side, the interesting parts come when the family's walk becomes threatened by a never-ending set of obstacles. First, there's 'long wavy grass', then a 'deep cold river', then 'thick oozy mud'. Each time the family come across a new obstacle, a phrase repeats: 'We can't go over it. We can't go under it. Oh no! We've got to go through it.' And that, right there, is motherhood. You cannot cheat the newborn days. You cannot skip over the uncertainty. You can't burrow under the exhaustion. You have to go through it. Except, at the end of your story, instead of a grizzly bear hiding in a cave, there is an adored, deliciously scruffy toddler saying 'OK, lub you, bye bye bye,' to some sausages.

When you hear a new mother say, '*Why did no one tell me how hard this would be?*', it's easy to assume she spent her formative years in the wilderness being raised by a family of badgers, only meeting humans aged 28 when a kindly farmer took her in and taught her about important human things like Kit Kats and Dermot O'Leary. *How* can she not have known? The fact that the newborn stage can be utterly and appallingly dreadful is a universally known truth, isn't it? Who on Earth did she get her information from when she was pregnant? People with kids who were stone-cold liars? People *without* kids who told her new babies are no more demanding than a hamster?

When a first-time parent complains that their gruelling experience of the newborn stage came as a shock, what I think they're really saying is, 'OK, I never expected it to be a day at the beach, but why did no one sit me down and drum it into me? And I mean *really* drum it in. Grab me by the shoulders and look me square in the eye while forcing me to sign a document in my own blood that states I fully acknowledge the potential horror that awaits. That I, New Parent, am willingly signing up to a brutal existential upheaval accompanied with a tiredness so engulfing I will happily offer up my child to Beelzebub himself if it means I can float down into the depths of sleep for another 15 blissful seconds?'

While pregnant, I would scoff at those 'shocked' new mums. 'HA! Wallies!' I would think, rubbing my bump smugly. 'Imagine being surprised that the first few months are hard. They should have been more like *me*. Me who has read and listened to *everything*. Me, who's grilled everyone I can think of, insisting they linger on the gory details and provide photos where possible. I am incredibly well prepared. Nothing can surprise me!' And yet, if I'm honest, in spite of the frequent traumatising tales my interrogations would force from existing mums, I couldn't shake off a hunch that I was, in fact, so special, *whispers* *that I would be exempt from any newborn horror.*

A close friend would be sharing a story about the darkness of their baby blues, when, midway through them sobbing at a memory of having a breakdown in the homeware section of TK Maxx when their buggy clipped a shelf and knocked off a Le Creuset lasagne dish, my vain internal monologue would begin. Just like in a movie, I would slowly tune out from what my friend was saying and only hear the deeply misguided but utterly alluring lies my own ego was teasing me with. 'Don't listen to her,' it would purr, 'Yes, newborns are hard for *some* people, Ellie, but not for you. Have you forgotten that you are the centre of the universe? You will be the *exception*! *You* will be fine! You will endure. You, Ellie . . . are a *warrior.*' The voice would pause here for maximum emphasis, before whispering, 'After all, you have completed the . . . *Duke of Edinburgh Silver Award . . .*' And with that mic drop, the voice would evaporate, and I'd be back with my friend. There I would sit, silently pitying their weakness from which I would be spared because when I was 16, I'd spent three days trekking in the Brecon Beacons with quite a nasty blister.

Ultimately, it doesn't really matter what you think before-hand. Regardless of whether you anticipate newborn life to be utterly awful or 100% pure ROFLs, you will be wrong. Whatever your expectation, the reality is likely to be a totally different experience to the one you'd imagined. Like attempting to describe what wasabi tastes like before you've ever tried it. You cannot know what life with a newborn is like until you have had a newborn. Then, and only then, can you really know. And Christ, *then you really know.*

I think I first began to properly 'know' at around 3.00 am
on our first night back from hospital. The baby was crying.
I had fed her. I had changed her. I had cuddled her. The
baby was still crying. I had used up every weapon in my
extremely limited armoury. What the hell was I meant to do
now? The best course of action, I decided, was to take the
baby, leave the bedroom and then wander the dark house with
the screaming two-day-old creature in my arms. In hindsight,
I realise that this thinking was down to the fact it seemed like
the kind of thing a 'new mum' character would do in a
romcom. Presumably, any minute now, a shirtless Matthew
McConaughey would appear to sway the baby to sleep via
some skin-to-skin and an adorable crooning rendition of 'It
Had to be You'. It makes sense to me now, that my tired
strange little brain went straight to film-esque portrayals of
new motherhood because brief on-screen fictionalised scenes
were the only time I'd ever glimpsed a newborn night. *Daytime*
with the baby, I had a vague understanding of what to expect.
We've all seen a mum in the park looking like crap and pushing
a shiny new pram. We've all seen two new parents in a café
taking it in turn to inhale a panini before struggling to slip
their tiny screaming worm of a baby into a sling. We recog-
nise that. We've witnessed that. Daytime is, to some degree,
a known entity, but night times were a blank page.

Obviously, I'd heard the nights were bad. Who hasn't, but
I'll say it again – *you can't know until you know* – and I wish
I had known a little more. If only one of my NCT classes
had involved a field trip to a new mum's house in the middle
of the night to watch her be woken for a fifth time in as
many hours. From the shadows, witness her being dragged
from the blackest depths of the deepest sleep, wrenched to

the surface of consciousness by a screaming cacophony. Feeling deranged with tiredness, she rips open her eyes and then her bra, or fumbles to prepare some formula. The baby finds what it needs, and for the moment, there is silence. Have you ever been woken up in a hotel by a fire alarm? Heart racing, confusion, temporary loss of knowing who or where you are? That is what I would have seen. A woman drunk with exhaustion, struggling to remember her child's name. Struggling to remember her own.

As I wandered cluelessly around my house on that first wild night, Matthew McConaughey nowhere in sight, I eventually found myself lying on the living room floor, my crying baby next to me. After only 48 hours, it was apparent that mothering was, in fact, perhaps *even harder* than the Duke of Edinburgh Silver Award. I'd been inducted into the most savage organisation ever created: The Newborn Night Club. The nights where the world turns on its head and your own bedroom becomes the thing that scares you most in the world. The nights where you wake with a start and begin frantically ripping back the covers convinced you've lost the baby in the bedding only to see them sleeping quietly in their cot. Or, like my friend Anna, the nights where you wake to find you are so delirious you have been attempting to swaddle your husband's foot. The nights where you sit with your feeding baby, urging 4.30 am to come around so you can take solace in the fact that somewhere across London, Ben Shephard will be in a taxi on his way to the set of *Good Morning Britain*, so that you can feel less alone.

I remember looking at my daughter on that first night as she squirmed next to me on the floor, her face right by mine, both of us eerily lit by the streetlamp outside. One overwhelming thought repeated in my head, 'I have absolutely no idea what I am doing. *Why did no one tell me how hard this would be?'*

Those first weeks were bleaker than an episode of *The Handmaid's Tale*. I was told I would likely get the baby blues for a few days after the birth, feeling teary as my hormones recalibrated and sent my brain off a cliff, but in my case, these blues seemed to hang around. I hoped I would grow to love my baby, but for now, my feelings remained around the 'like/ feel responsibility towards'. Not only was I dealing with my physical pain but also a terrifying wave of postnatal emotions that assured me having my daughter was a cataclysmic error. I cried all the time, for no reason and every reason all at once. I would silently and sometimes loudly berate myself for falling for humanity's sick trick: making people think becoming a parent is a life-affirming part of our ultimate destiny. 'There is nothing life-affirming about this,' I thought, as I wept in bed, wearing the same pair of knickers I'd been in for three days straight. 'This is *awful*. I should have got a cat. Why didn't I get a cat!?' At which point my chin would tremble, and the tears would once again begin to rain down on my enormous leaky boobs as I mourned the loss of a tabby I'd never know and, crucially, would never have to breastfeed 20 times a day.

I look back now and wonder if my sense of being marooned in those first few months was just regular baby blues or if I was the one in ten women who experience postnatal depression in the first year of their child's life. The fact is, many women fall through the cracks when having their PND diagnosed. No professional would have noticed with me. Outwardly,

I was functioning – I attended all the relevant baby appointments on time, wearing a smile and, occasionally, mascara. But my mind felt undeniably scrambled. I would urge any woman who is feeling odd to talk to her GP. And if that seems too formal, like it did for me, start smaller and begin by speaking to someone who loves you. It can be terrifying to say out loud that you don't feel right, especially if you've never had any mental health issues before, but there is help out there. There is no need to feel ashamed or frightened. No one is going to think you're a bad mum if you reveal that something is a bit off-kilter. You've just got a poorly brain that needs time, space and perhaps some medicine to get better. But you will get better, my love, you will.

My saving grace here was my husband. (For any woman who has done the newborn bit solo, you have my absolute enduring respect. When the inevitable nuclear Armageddon happens, there is no group of people I'd like to hide in a cave and rebuild civilisation with more.) Phil was a textbook wonderful partner and an exceptional servant. He showed such stoic compassion as he cooked and cleaned around me, ensuring I was fed, watered and mollycoddled, that I began to call him Dobby after the house elf in *Harry Potter*. I said that if he was lucky, when Ratbag was 18 years old, I would throw him a nursing bra to release him from his servitude (if you don't get that reference, then shame on you). He also had the unenviable task of being my in-house nurse – meaning that for ten days after I arrived home from hospital he had to administer blood clot prevention injections. Every evening the bedroom door would creak open, and there he'd be, backlit, the silhouette of a man holding a syringe slowly stalking towards a sobbing woman in bed crying out, 'No, no, please no!', except this villain always apologised profusely, before making his victim a green smoothie.

Another role I made Dobby take on was that of 'misery archiver'. I insisted he take photos, but not just the standard ones. I wanted the whole spectrum documented. So, while there are plenty of 'mother holding child and smiling' snaps on his camera roll, I also made him capture me at my lowest. Crying and broken, sitting on the floor struggling to use a breast pump as the first edges of an infection crept in. 'I need to remember,' I insisted. 'If I don't remember, I might think about doing it again. And. I. Am. *Never*. Doing. This. Again.'

For a good while after I had my daughter, though I cared for her tenderly – kissing her crusty little head as she fed – I knew with absolute certainty that she had ruined my life.

I talked to my mum while writing this newborn chapter, confessing how I was worried it was all darkness and, not enough light. She said, 'You didn't find it all *that* bad, did you?'. 'Mum,' I said, 'The first few months were horrendous.' She laughed. 'No, it wasn't!' she said, brushing off the comment as she cheerfully reflected on newborn life with her own first baby, my sister, Shona. Once she'd finished, I had to quietly remind her that this chirpy retelling wasn't strictly true. I knew my parents had undertaken an international move from Hong Kong back to the UK when my sister was 12 weeks old, that they'd rented a flat in an area of London where they had no friends and that postnatal depression settled in soon after.

As I repeated back the facts as I knew them, she admitted that, yes, all of that was true, but to band it all together and label newborn life with my sister as 'awful' felt disloyal to her little baby girl who is now a 40-year-old marathon runner. I said to my mum, just as I say to every first-time mother whom I pounce on in the park, that it's entirely possible to like/love your newborn baby but to simultaneously hate the newborn experience. Admitting to finding it hard does not cast aspersions on your child's character, neither does it undermine your gratitude at being able to have a child nor question your ability to parent. When my daughter is older, I will happily tell her how atrocious our time together was at the beginning, hoping that if one day she decides to have children, she will feel able to admit the same to her dear, old, incredibly stylish mum. So, for anyone reading this who's harbouring shame about their negative reflections on early parenting, then I say this loudly for you:

I LOVE MY DAUGHTER. I LOVE HER WITH A PASSION I HAVE NEVER PREVIOUSLY EXPERIENCED, BUT NEWBORN LIFE WITH HER FUCKING SUCKED. IT SUCKED BIG HAIRY SWEATY BUM. IT WAS AWFUL AND RELENTLESS AND I WANTED IT AND HER TO PISS OFF SO I COULD SLEEP OR HAVE A WANDER AROUND RIVER ISLAND. I WANTED THIS FOR MONTHS AND MONTHS. SOMETIMES I STILL WANT IT NOW. IF ANYONE SAYS ANYTHING DIFFERENT, THEY ARE TELLING HUGE FUCKING FIBS.

The best way to describe my newborn outlook was that everything just felt *wrong*. I knew that technically the world I was in now was the same world in which I'd fallen asleep in a Vue cinema while Eddie Redmayne burped at me, and yet it felt like everything had somehow shifted. My feelings towards, and my relationship with, everything had been scrambled. As though my old life had been tipped into a NutriBullet, blended up, and then the contents, molecularly the same but now unrecognisable, had been poured back out. And that was that. I knew that my house was the same home, my husband was the same man, and my marriage was the same relationship, but it was all twisted and blurry, like I was looking at it all underwater. I couldn't decipher how I now existed. How did I slot back in after a child had been lifted from me – plucked out of my body like a pin pulled from a grenade creating invisible devastation on a scale I could not grasp?

I felt as if I was physically living in one place but existing somewhere totally other. I would sit in a daze in front of the telly, tits flopped out, with a child feeding from me and think to myself, 'How can I possibly watch TV like everything is fine? How can *anyone* be watching TV when my life is destroyed? How can the universe continue? How can *Gogglebox*'s Giles and Mary sit there eating Ferrero Rocher and making sardonic comments about Bradley Walsh when I am questioning how to just fucking *be*?'

I realise now the saddest thing is that while I felt so down, I was unable to be thankful for what I did have – a perfect newborn, my own physical health, a warm house, a caring partner. I was living under a sheet of darkness that obliterated everything good. That's the cruel thing about baby blues or postnatal depression or whatever combination of the two I had – it affords you no joy. I hated the world. I hated the fact that the house was so dark and joyless. I hated the fact I felt insane. I hated how everything seemed overwhelming, even the most simple of tasks. My phone ringing would cause adrenalin to surge through my body like I'd just leapt off a skyscraper.

Showers had to be undertaken at warp speed in case my boobs were required elsewhere, and opportunities to blow dry my hair became as frequent as an appearance from Halley's Comet. Even something as basic as having a poo ended up being a traumatic ordeal.

I think every woman's first poo after she's had a baby is something they will remember almost as clearly as their child's birth. Sadly, though, it doesn't garner you as many 'Welcome to the World!' Moonpig cards. My first poo was five days after I'd had my daughter. The urge came while I was midway through feeding my child (to be honest, at this point, I was always midway through feeding my child). Too scared to put her down and risk a screaming fit, I took my daughter into the bathroom, locked the door, pulled down my gargantuan pants, and sat on the toilet.

Now, there are a few things to know at this point.

Firstly, after you've had a baby, it's very common for your digestive system to give itself a well-deserved bit of R&R as it deals with kamikaze hormones and a shrinking giant uterus. Secondly, if you've had a C-section, you also have the remnants of drugs from surgery doing strange things to your insides – the same insides that are recovering from being kneaded by a surgeon like an enriched dough. All in all, the general internal vibe is, 'Thanks for riding the Bowel Train – next stop, Constipation Station. We apologise for delays to our regular service – this is due to congestion in the small intestine area.'

I sat on the throne, babe in arms – a modern take on the Madonna and Child. I considered my tactics. I knew that my surgically separated stomach muscles were still exceptionally weak because every time I coughed, it felt like my scar would burst open and ooze out my innards like an M&S melt-in-the-middle pudding. I was also very aware that ahead of the baby's arrival, we'd had the bathroom floor redone with some fancy Moroccan tiles that were very pretty but also highly porous. There was no way I was letting some rogue guts leave a stain.

I hunched forward, clutching my stomach in an attempt to reinforce my abdomen with a single hand since my other hand was still busy holding the happily dining Ratbag. I braced myself. The urge was now urgent. I knew this was to be an epic battle. I began sweating. I gritted my teeth and tried to remember all the tips I'd learnt from the one article on hypnobirthing I'd skim-read. I silently bore down, counting to ten over and over, and pushing, pushing, pushing – like a hippo delivering breech twins. Then suddenly and all at once, the Kraken burst forth, landing with a heavy thud and catapulting water over my bum cheeks like a sea mine had just been detonated in the U-bend. I sat there panting, certain there could be nothing left inside me because I'd just shat out everything my torso had ever housed. I must now be a mere husk – a drinking straw of human skin. I may have had my daughter via my abdomen but I now felt I knew what it was like to birth something from the other end. I remained there, recovering, delighted that the dreadful assault was over. I checked my stomach was still glued up and then slowly manoeuvred myself into an upright position with the baby still feeding. There. I was standing. I'd done it. Well done, Ellie! I hit the flush.

Oh god . . . Ohgod Ohgod Ohgod . . . I watched as the water swirled over the unmoving monster giving it nothing more than a tickle. It hadn't flinched. 'Don't panic!' I thought, 'It's just a two-flusher. Nothing to worry about. Stay calm.'

Reader, it wasn't a two flusher. It wasn't even a three flusher.

There was another problem. My husband and I have a very frank relationship. He happily lets me go on stage in front of thousands of people and divulge all sorts of embarrassing, intimate information. I once did a whole stand-up tour based around how I wish I could have sex with men who aren't my husband. He saw this show countless times, and at every gig, he guffawed loudly at his horny-clown of a wife. But despite the openness between us, one subject that has remained steadfastly in our marriage's 'conversational no-fly zone' is anything to do with bathroom activities. My strange prudish attempt at clutching onto the last fibres of our now totally threadbare cloak of mystery. At this point in our marriage, I had barely even said the word 'poo' in Phil's presence and vice versa – to this day, I'm still not entirely sure he even has a sphincter. So, as I stood in that bathroom, I knew it would be like going from 0-100mph if I were to now suddenly yell down the stairs, 'Phil, can you come up here? In a bit of a bind . . .'

No. No help was coming. I was going to have to save myself.

After a fourth unsuccessful flush, I had a moment of inspiration (if you can still have inspiration when you've barely slept for five days and are 75% unhinged). I decided that the obvious course of action was to open the bathroom cabinet, fish out a clear plastic shower cap I'd stolen from a hotel, put it over my fingers like a protective mitten and physically break up my giant unrelenting turd with my own hand. And that is what I did. While in considerable physical pain, and with my child never breaking her latch. Feel free to give me a remote high five if you wish (please sanitise thoroughly afterwards). I flushed the loo again and watched as my shame was finally swept away.

We all know the saying, 'Not all heroes wear capes', but it's also important to include the rarely quoted follow-up line, 'Some heroes wear a shit-covered shower cap glove that they secretly dispose of in the nappy bin'.

Coincidentally, at a recent baby shower for a friend, I began swapping war stories with another woman who had also had a C-section. I told her my ridiculous poo story, and it turned out that her first post-birth poop had also resulted in a non-flushing behemoth. However, while I'd gone down the tried and tested 'chop it up with your index finger and thumb in a pincer movement' route, she had chosen to pluck her poo out from the toilet bowl with a plastic bag which she then wrapped inside several more plastic bags like some kind of horrific pass-the-parcel game. She then gave the package to her husband accompanied with the words, 'Don't ask me what is in here, just put it in the outside bin.' He did as she asked, and to this day, he has never mentioned it. To quote Salt and indeed Pepa, 'What a mighty, mighty good man'.

In the midst of this shitty period of my life, I found a glimmer of hope in the unlikely form of my boobs. As I said earlier, in my old existence, my bazongas were unremarkable and unfeeling, but as milk makers, they turned out to be absolute Super Soaker stars. Now, before I bang on about how great my bangers were, let me state here that I am a firm believer that, as long as a baby is fed, it doesn't matter what vessel the milk is provided in. I had always hoped to breastfeed, so that is the route I went down, whereas my sister, for instance, wasn't mad on the idea (and also had a rough time with it – a common problem that I'll get into shortly), so her kids were formula munchers. I remember once talking to another mother about the interminable breast vs bottle chat and her saying to me, 'Imagine a school nativity play – a stage full of angels and wise men picking their noses – can you tell which kids were breastfed and which had formula?' Of course, you can't. Yes, that's an extremely reductive way of looking at it, but my opinion is, as long as you don't give your newborn a double macchiato, they're going to be fine. Feed your babe whichever way makes you all the happiest.

But back to my bangers. As soon as Ratbag met my breasts, they got on like long lost pals, and I was delighted because I knew nursing a child seems all too often fraught with issues. I have known many friends end their breastfeeding attempts abruptly due to lack of milk or unsuited latches. Some endured bleeding ravaged nipples, infections and abscesses, and therefore some of them, understandably, could bear it no longer and cut their journey short. Breastfeeding is a skill that needs to be learnt by both mother and child, and sometimes, down to no fault of anyone involved, even after seeking help, it just doesn't work out. In those cases, I have known some mothers move on to formula very pragmatically, while others have tormented themselves over it. If that is you as you stare at your six-month-old asleep on your chest or you harbour regret about how your now 14-year-old, who is sneering at you from under a heavy fringe, was fed in that first year, then I hope you know that in the grand scheme of things, *it's such small biccies*. Continuing with something that is easy is, in itself, easy, whereas calling quits on something you really want to do? That is a much trickier path to take. There's bravery there, in that decision.

Through sheer luck, my boobs decided to play ball. That's not to say there weren't a few bumpy patches along my nursing path. Quite literally, during a few run-ins with mastitis, when my boobs became lumpy, red, fiery hot boulders.

The whole concept of mastitis infuriates me. It is an unthinkably cruel move on behalf of nature that it's even a thing. It felt like I was being trolled by the heavens. 'Look at her, down there – the unwashed crazed one in the dirty Primark nightdress. God, she looks awful, doesn't she? Never stops bloody crying and shouting at *Gogglebox*. You know what would be a laugh? If, while she felt this crap, we infect one of her tits!'

Having mastitis (which happened a few times #blessed) was the most unwell I have ever felt. A combination of intense flu, fever and hallucinations with the added spice of still having a tiny human who needs to physically drain the life force from your body every couple of hours. The first time I got sick was around week three, and we decided to call in a lactation consultant to see if the reason I'd run into trouble was to do with my baby's latch. We looked online and found a professional nearby who said she'd be able to help. Within a few hours, the doorbell rang.

As I sat delirious on the sofa, in walked a willowy American lady who we'll call Barbara, who was around 200 years old and wearing glasses with lenses as thick as custard creams. Barbara took a seat, asked me a few questions and proceeded to open a small suitcase she'd brought with her. After some scrabbling around, she found what she was looking for – which turned out to be a hand puppet of much loved Sesame Street character, Elmo. If the next thing that happened hadn't been captured on Phil's phone as part of his 'misery archive' I would have put it down to another mastitis-related hallucination. Barbara put the puppet on her hand, came over to where I was sitting, and placed Elmo to my breast. She then proceeded to use poor innocent Elmo to demonstrate different feeding positions and explain how my baby's mouth should look while sucking (which was apparently open to around 180 degrees and surrounded by bright red fur). Even demented with fever, I remember looking down at my naked top half as she manoeuvred Elmo into the 'rugby ball hold' and thinking, 'Well, this is absolutely bats'. Whenever I reflect on this strange encounter (which is more often than you'd think), I am always left with the same searing question: 'Am I relieved or disappointed that the puppet was Elmo and not the Cookie Monster?' Actually, who am I kidding? I'm *gravely* disappointed. From a personality point of view, a character with a famed hunger is the obvious choice – plus, can you imagine how much fun you could have if you adapted his catchphrase from 'Mmmmm cookie' to 'Mmmmm boobie'? Such a missed opportunity. It will not come as a shock to hear that we never saw Barbara or Elmo again.

Once I stopped getting ill, nursing was working out well. For starters, it meant none of my energy needed to be spent washing, sterilising and preparing bottles of formula. What a win! I could instead just focus on breastfeeding my exclusively breastfed baby. Now, if that sounds like a smug sentence, then let me draw your attention to the main flaw in having an exclusively breastfed baby, which is that, by definition, it requires the person with the breasts to exclusively handle every feed.

Every single feed.

Every few hours.

All day.

All night.

I did this dutifully for weeks. I was soon a woman standing

dutifully on the edge. Eventually, after having not slept for more than three hours in a row for two months, we decided to switch one of the evening feeds to a bottle so that Phil could take charge while I slept. The plan went ahead, I slept for six hours, and the baby was nonchalant about the whole thing. The morning after, I kept saying how brilliant it was and that I didn't know why we hadn't used some formula sooner. This, however, was a lie. I knew exactly why I hadn't used formula, and the reasons were:

1) In my strange mental state, I had found a sense of pride in my exhaustion. My natural stubbornness had been listening intently to the all-pervading 'breast is best' message and linked breaking my unbroken streak of only feeding my daughter breast milk with 'failure'. I'd fallen into the trap.

2) Because breastfeeding was the magic trick that only I, the enchanting nork-wielding sorceress, could perform. If someone else could feed her, it meant that I was replaceable and could lose my position as doyenne of this new parenting racket. I was like Gollum, lusting for something that, in turn, was driving me mad.

3) Because while I despised the exhaustion and claustrophobia that came with the constant feeding, I came to treasure the act itself. Nursing my cub, sitting quietly as this tiny being folded her body around mine, a miniature yin to my yang.

Over that first year, the ratio of bottle feeds my baby had would gradually begin to outweigh the feeds directly from my tit taps. By the time the babe was eight months old, my milk was beginning to dwindle just as her teeth were appearing. It was time for the breastaurant to cease trading. I am so glad I was able to feed her for that long, and if I have another child, I would happily aim to breastfeed again, but this time with a caveat. The caveat being that I would make sure that from the very beginning, I would palm off a couple of bottle feeds to my husband quicker than a middle-class woman booking her Christmas Ocado slot. How lucky we are to live in a time where science gives us the option to outsource milk provision, and how I wish the prickly conversation about feeding babies wasn't so binary. Contrary to the vast majority of discourse on the subject, you don't have to pick team Breast or Bottle, get it branded on your forehead and live with that choice forever. There is a middle ground of combination feeding that shares the load for everyone. Babies are lovely, and if you're able to, breastfeeding can be too. But you know what's even lovelier? A new mum getting six hours sleep.

There is a word for this period of a woman's life when she becomes a mother – 'matrescence' – a phrase coined in 1975 by anthropologist Dana Raphael in her book, *Being Female: Reproduction, Power and Change*. In the same way adolescence is the tumultuous process of becoming an adult, matrescence, Raphael explains, is the hormonal, physical and psychological process that a woman undergoes as she becomes a mother. This rings vast Big Ben-style bells for me. So much focus is put on the birth and the baby that the mother's transformation during that 'fourth trimester' is often overlooked and never named. *Of course* I felt peculiar – I was going through the biggest existential evolution of my life. Where was that in the sodding NCT curriculum, Janet? An hour playing 'zip zap boing' and yet zero time dedicated to a discussion on the fundamental mind-bending adjustment that waited ahead?

What I was very lucky to have was a support system, even if I couldn't see it clearly at the time. Thanks in large part to the huge cast of women who cared for me in ways big and small, I gradually began to adjust. I clearly remember collapsing onto my mum one day when my daughter was a few months old.

'It's just so hard' I cried, over and over. 'It's so, so hard.' She took me in her arms and held me like the baby I will always be to her. She stroked my face and said exactly what every new mum wants to hear – no attempt at tough love or a 'buck up' speech, instead she offered empathy and, more importantly, hope.

'It *is* hard, Ellie,' she said. 'You're finding it hard because it is exactly that, and you are doing such a brilliant job, darling, you really are. It won't be like this forever. I promise you that.'

Every day my incredible mother, my wonderful sister and a legion of other mums picked me up and began to put me back together. Daily messages, from people that ranged from close friends to women I barely knew, strengthened and soothed me. They had all had a baby, they had survived, and because of them, I knew I would too. They dragged me through whatever I was experiencing and lifted me to the surface. There were a hundred small acts of kindness; a cuddle, a call, a 'just checking in' text, each added another breath of air into a life float that would carry me safely to the other side.

The bad news is, because of all those angelic women, when I see a new mum nowadays, I am like a moth to an emotionally vulnerable flame. God forbid I met you once in 2004 and I find out you're now up the duff because I'll be sliding into your DMs before you can say, 'BLOCK'. I adore new magical mums with a burning passion because, while I know how broken they can be, I now have the newfound knowledge that they will heal. I chat up new mums everywhere – on the street, in cafés, or in my most successful hunting ground – the baby department of John Lewis. I do it so often I even have a go-to opening line. I sidle over to the woman, look at the baby in their pram and say, 'Ooh – that one looks fresh!' The mum usually laughs because she's fragile and BOOM, I've wangled my way in. I ask how sleep is going and say, 'Oh, you poor thing,' as they recount the abysmal night they've just had. I enquire how feeding is working out and, if relevant, I scribble on an old receipt the number of the great lactation expert I found after I parted ways with Elmo. I tell them they look wonderful and that they *are* wonderful, and as I wish them farewell, I always say the same thing: 'It does get better, you know. It may not seem like it right now, but it really, really will. I promise you that.'

My 'better' came when my baby was heading towards five months old. Day by day, I realised that I was smiling more than I was crying during my trips to Tesco. I began to stop feeling like I was wading through fog and acting as a version of myself. I stopped having to run things through my brain like a computer to check that the action I was about to undertake was the kind of thing that 'the character of Ellie Taylor' would say or watch or eat.

I had a realisation that up until this point, I'd been treating parenting as if it were a project with an end date. I'd been living in a constant state of, 'If I can just get through to Tuesday/Thursday/the weekend . . .' as if when the days came

I'd be able to hand in a dissertation and then head to Mykonos for ten days of sun and frozen daiquiris. The realisation, and I mean the *true* realisation, that *there is no end*, that there is no deadline, that this existence is not a short-term temporary burst of graft but rather a new way of living was obvious and at the same time revelatory to me. Rather than greeting the night-time disruptions, the unpredictability and the tiredness with resentment and withdrawal as I scrabbled furiously towards a finish line that didn't exist, I instead started to try to embrace this new role of mine.

I distinctly remember the moment it clicked. It was the middle of the night, and I was putting Ratbag back in her cot after a feed. She was crying and wouldn't settle. I was so tired I felt like crying too, but instead, I found my brain having a word with myself. 'Ellie,' it said, 'For the moment, this, your daughter, is your job. Forget everything else. She needs you. Lean into it. You can do this. Now do your job.'

And I did.

And I do.

You can't go over it.

You can't go under it.

You have to go through it.

I I

Firsts

Just as the final stages of pregnancy provide a list of 'lasts', the initial 12 months of your baby's life presents you with an influx of 'firsts'. And let me be clear, I'm not talking about the baby here. The baby gets enough attention for their accomplishments, thank you very much – you can barely move on a new mum WhatsApp group for photos of gurning witchetty grubs next to laminated milestone cards saying: 'Today I smiled for the first time!' (As I wrote this, I thought what a savvy business idea it would be to create some alternative versions of these baby cards, saying things like, 'Today I ate some gravel!', or, 'Today I scratched Mummy's cornea and she had to go to A&E!', but I've just checked Etsy and can confirm that that gap in the market is very much filled.)

No, the firsts I am talking about here are the experiences that *parents* will go through – a multitude of fresh achievements and disasters that range from the tiny to the massive, each one a tick off the list and another step away from the 'miraculous' (and appalling) newborn days.

In the first few weeks, you'll be doing new things for the first time every day. From the very first time you change a nappy ('Cute! Look how tiny it is!'). Less cute a couple of years in when changes become wrestling matches with a shit-covered python), to your first post-birth shower (absolute heaven as long as you don't examine anything too closely – never have the words 'don't look down' been so relevant), to the first time you use a baby carrier and accidentally bend the baby's leg back to an unholy angle (don't worry – you won't do it again. Probably).

Then there's the first time you wear proper clothes (although there's no rush there – I was in my maternity gear for a good few months because I like both stretchiness *and* shortbread which is coincidentally the name of my favourite 90s garage duo) or the first time you introduce your child as '. . . my son/daughter' (even more thrilling than the time I named Daniel Barns my 'boyfriend' after my Year 6 'punk' themed school disco where my ripped fishnets made me look like a participant in a Lady of the Night apprenticeship scheme).

My *big* 'first' came around a week or so after I'd arrived home, and it was the 'first time I fed in public'. At this point, it had been a good 15 years since I'd last been bare-breasted in front of strangers (in a bar in Magaluf, involving sambuca as opposed to a small café and a vegetable quiche). As with many things concerning parenting, the prospect turned out to be far worse than the reality. I sat down at a table, lifted up my top, unclipped my nursing bra and hooked the bairn up to the milk keg. No one noticed or cared. My babe was simply having lunch while I had mine. Within a few weeks, I became so at ease with whipping out my breasts in that café, I'm confident that still to this day, the barista could identify my areolae in a police line-up.

I always felt very comfortable feeding my baby in public wherever and whenever I needed to, largely because I am extremely stubborn, and if nothing else, there was a point of principle to uphold. I always approached it as a matter of fact: 'Right, well, she needs to eat. Better unleash one of the lads then.' In the hundreds of feeds I gave while out and about, I never experienced any of the outrage you occasionally read about online where a mother has been asked to leave a premises or told to cover up. I was always secretly hoping someone would say something so I could flex my sanctimonious muscles, but no. Nothing. I began to wonder if I'd had a lucky ride, so I asked my breastfeeding friends about their experiences, but it turned out none of them have ever been on the receiving end of any public outrage either – aside from the time a pal's little one was going nuts on a packed bus, and a man helpfully yelled at her to, 'Shove your tit in its mouth to shut it up!' which is, in its own way, aggressively pro-breastfeeding. Well done to that angry man for his open-minded verbal assault.

The next sizeable 'first' I faced was much more daunting than a simple bit of al fresco nip action. It was the big one – 'the first day alone with the baby'. Phil, using a combination of holiday and official paternity leave (the standard paltry UK allowance of two weeks, but we'll get into more of that later) had been lucky to have over a month at home with our daughter. Soon enough, though, it was time for him to return to work. Off he went, my little Dobby all suited and booted, waving us goodbye; sad to leave but delighted to be able to have a Leon chicken burger for lunch. (On a similar note, my 'first bite of a Pret meatball wrap' after I had the baby was one of the most searingly erotic experiences of my life.)

In a bid to keep busy on our first full solo girl's day, I took Ratbag on a trip to a big shopping mall where my girl did a violent all-up-the-back-poo in Waitrose that resulted in me binning all the clothes she was wearing and buying new ones. If you haven't got a story involving a sentence along the lines of, '. . . so then I had to push her around Next wrapped in an old sheet I found in the boot', have you even had a baby?

From this point in parenting, the poo stories (much like the poos themselves) come thick and fast. Before long, you'll have notched up tales involving all the various bodily fluids, and the older the child gets, the more spectacular they become and the less you care. For instance, when Ratbag was about seven months old and well on her solid food journey, I met up with a friend in a vegan café where my child, keen to prove her great sense of irony, projectile vomited lots of very cheese-heavy puke all over the floor. It was awful. For starters, Comté is expensive, but worse than that, it was incredibly unpleasant and very yellow. People looked at me in both disgust and pity as I packed up and fled before you could say, 'Alfalfa and fennel smoothie'. Awkward does not cover it. But you know what, no one died (very on-brand for vegans) and all I kept thinking was that it still wasn't as bad as the time my friend's boyfriend vommed red wine all over my mum's beige sofa on New Year's Eve 2003. Sure, the café floor had been splattered by some regurgitated dairy, but that was nothing compared to gathering up lumps of Shiraz from down the back of a velveteen Laura Ashley love seat.

Talking of Shiraz, it's time to tackle the tastiest of all the firsts – the beautiful 'first post-birth booze'. This happened on about week two of motherhood for me, and I bestowed the honour on a can of M&S Mojito. For the whole two minutes that it lasted, I was no longer crying on a sofa. I was crying on a *tropical* sofa which, if you can ignore mosquitos, is much nicer.

This quickly led to another (slightly more concerning) new mum experience: 'The first day I had a glass of wine at 4.00 pm'. It was alarmingly easy for this to become a regular little treat. A gift to myself. 'To Me, well done on surviving another day! Here, have this liquid reward. Lots of love, Me xxx'. It was when I found myself, on one unremarkable Wednesday, finishing off my second vodka at 6.00 pm thinking, 'Wow. I feel so much better. Maybe I just need to drink more,' that I thought I should perhaps knock it on the head.

The gin-swilling-stay-at-home-mum is a well-trodden stereotype, and one that I've often rolled my eyes at in depictions of new motherhood for being lazy and hack. I take it all back – it's not a stereotype; it's gritty realism. Yes, there are some lovely bits of maternity leave, but the good parts (gurgles, binging *The Crown*, putting your kid in jumpers that have rabbit ears on the hood) make up around 15% of the experience, with the other 85% reserved for grinding monotony. New mums are looking down the barrel at months, perhaps years, of sometimes lovely but often boring, lonely, tedious days. It's hardly surprising, then, that on another Groundhog Day of solitude that started at 4.00 am, by 4.00 pm a mum may look at a can of G&T and think, 'Well hello, old friend! Come! Sit down, stay a while!'.

If breastfeeding itself is a spiky subject, then breastfeeding and drinking booze is a hedgehog who shaved their legs four days ago with a blunt Venus. Some nursing mums abstain completely whereas others have a few tipples occasionally, perhaps adhering to the 'pump and dump' line of thought. It's a personal choice each woman will make based on the facts she seeks out, but whatever school of thought you may follow, it's fair to say that getting shitfaced when you have a newborn is never going to be a great idea no matter which way you're feeding your child.

In my case, after going to a specific NCT class on breast-feeding and asking lots of questions along the lines of, 'So how many Pornstar Martinis is *too* many, would you say?' I decided that while binge drinking certainly wasn't on the agenda for a while, I was comfortable having a couple of drinks every so often while maintaining my new role as 'human buffet'. (Just to be Sensible Sally for a minute, drinking any amount of alcohol and co-sleeping, or falling asleep with the baby on a sofa or chair is never OK. If you have had a big blow-out make sure there is an uninebriated adult to care for the baby and, also, *you*, because my god, a hangover with a baby results in Stephen King levels of horror.)

Instead of booze (or perhaps I should say, as well as booze), some stay-at-home parents fight the tedium by filling their days with endless catch-ups and classes, becoming their child's PA, busy facilitating a hectic and varied social life. I, on the other hand, was far too neurotic for that sense of adventure. In general, I found it easier if I kept the days small and my ambitions low. Having no plans meant I could never be late or let anyone down, which made me feel less on edge. I'm a happily solitary person by nature and spent many a day during my maternity leave aimlessly cruising the streets with the pram, notching up thousands of steps while my ears gobbled up audiobook, after playlist, after podcast. Who needs face-to-face interaction when you can listen to an episode of *Woman's Hour* in which they discuss the history of the wooden spoon?

In hindsight, though, it probably would have been better for me to have been a little more loosey-goosey and actually seen real people as opposed to living my life via WhatsApp. I was so focused on Ratbag having a routine, I let it chain me to the house. This may have also been linked to feeling low or anxious. It's a vicious cycle. If you're feeling lonely or isolated or are suffering from PND, this may, in turn, lead you to be too overwhelmed to go to the very places that help ease those exact feelings. No, of course your eight-week-old isn't remotely bothered about sitting in a circle with another load of knackered mums and babies while a weary version of 'sleeping bunnies' echoes around the community centre, but those sessions are just as much about the parent getting some positive social interaction as they are about your child learning the Makaton for 'Polly Put the Kettle On'.

I would spend my days doing mental maths – my brain humming with awake times versus nap times: how long had my daughter fed for, when would the next feed be due, would I have enough time to get to the shop and back before she kicked off? Probably not. Well, in that case, I'll just stay at home.

I remember consciously trying to break free from this natural homing pigeon tendency when Ratbag was nine weeks old. I promised my parents that I would brave a trek to a fancy restaurant on the Thames to celebrate my mum's birthday. 'The first big adventure'. Like a suburban Shackleton embarking on an expedition, I packed up my kit (nappies, wipes, ice pick) and stepped out into the wastelands of Antarctica (the Jubilee line). I navigated the buggy on and off two different trains, involving a complicated interchange and a broken lift, before making it to the restaurant *early*. The sun was shining, my liquid eyeliner was freakishly symmetrical, and my babe laid peacefully in her buggy the whole way through lunch. What a day. I relaxed and enjoyed myself so much I even posted a sarcastic 'maternity leave is awful' Instagram story, complete with photo of my smug face quaffing lunchtime champs. I was a capable explorer who should get out more because this whole leaving the house thing was a breeze! Broken lift aside, this odyssey had been easier than a word search in a copy of *Take a Break*. I knocked back the last of the fizz, said farewell to my parents and began the reverse journey home.

We'd barely left the restaurant before her screaming began. Inconsolable tearless wails. I walked a little further, hoping the motion would send her off to sleep again. It didn't. I did an emergency boob stop in a café. That didn't help either. She was going absolutely and uncontrollably batshit for no obvious reason, and we were still 50 minutes away from home. And, just to add some extra frisson to the experience, it was now the evening rush hour. I pushed her through the narrow cobbled backstreets of London's Southbank, her furious little howls echoing off the tall buildings that lined our route, and eventually made it down into the depths of the underground station to stand with 1000 other people on the rammed platform. The last thing I wanted to do was continue this trip on a packed train, but unless I was happy to start a new life living in London Bridge station, I had no option but to get us home.

By the time a train came along that I could feasibly squeeze onto with my tank of a pram, I was now holding the screaming ball of fury in my arms. I rammed the buggy onto the tube bashing the legs of numerous silent professional passengers looking on at the despairing woman trying not to fall over as she stood, rocking her angry baby, wedged in on the heaving carriage trying not to hyperventilate.

I once had to fly home after a work event at a music festival in Switzerland. I was cataclysmically hungover and so hot and bothered that I had something approaching a panic attack just before boarding which inexplicably led to me taking all my clothes off in a toilet cubicle in Geneva airport and nearly missing my flight. And yet, this trip home with a screaming baby on the tube was still ten times worse than that horrific plane journey (where I puked twice and ended up listening to 'More Than Words' by Westlife on loop for two hours in an attempt to calm myself). There I stood, surfing the carriage using all the core strength I could muster after my recent C-section, desperately willing the train to bypass all the stops before ours. I clung to my wailing daughter and whispered a never-ending urgent rendition of 'You are my Sunshine' in her ear as a hundred pairs of judgemental eyes bore into me.

Once finally off the train and through my front door, I thought, 'This is why home is good. Home is safe. Home is quiet.' I sat on the sofa and started to research if it was possible to buy an electronic ankle tag that would administer a few volts if I ever attempted to leave my postcode again.

But, as the baby grew older, things slowly became more manageable; I became less anxious, and of course, I did venture out again. I began to be able to ask myself, 'What's the worst that can happen? She goes mental, I have to leave early, and she cries in the back of the car for half an hour while I sing weird and increasingly desperate verses of 'Old MacDonald' that result in me belting out the line: 'and on that farm there was a . . . turbot.' Is anyone dead at the end of that scenario? No? Great, then carry on.' Babies scream for no reason, and it's infuriating and terrifying, but they will all, at some point in their development, stop. Just like the toddler tantrum stage, those meltdowns, too, shall pass. As I assume will the tween rage that precedes the inevitable teenage revolt.

I have a WhatsApp group called The Midnight Commune made up of a few female friends who all have kids in which we spend the majority of the chat despairing about motherhood (we also have two other stock conversations on repeat – one that revolves around what new TV shows we're watching, and another that focuses on how old we look and whether we should get fringes). On a typical day when one or more of our respective children is being a little shit, we take it in turns to remind each other that, 'It's a phase. It's a phase. It's a phase.' If parenting were a product, then 'It's a phase' would be its accompanying slogan. And it applies to your state of mind and your life as a parent as much as it applies to changes in your offspring. *All of it is a phase.* One day, tomorrow, next week, next year, things will be different. You'll leave your house again, and you won't be on edge. You'll leave your house again, and you won't need a buggy. You'll leave your house again and won't have to worry about someone crapping themselves on the slide or throwing Upsy Daisy in a pond because you won't let them lick a wall. One day, you'll even leave your house again, just you and your partner, because lying in wait for you even if you can't see it yet is your 'first date night'.

Phil and I ticked this romantic and highly organised night of fun off the list when our baby was about four months old. To make it extra exotic, our destination was a shopping centre where my love and I grabbed each other's mitts and raced giddily to the central food court, where we sat next to a Spudulike opposite a Dorothy Perkins and drank a 5.00 pm bottle of warm Prosecco. *It was marvellous.* There we were.

Us. Just us. Not 'parents' but two humans who had once pointed at the other and said, 'You are funny and sexy and make nice risotto. I CHOOSE YOU.' We'd been there all along, of course, but I just couldn't see us through all the despair and back-to-back episodes of *Judge Rinder*.

I often hear parents giving themselves a hard time for going on date nights, specifically for some kid-free time, only to spend all evening talking about their kids. Now that I have a child, I think it would be mad if you did anything *but* that, especially at the beginning. *Of course* Phil and I were going to spend our few hours together talking about our babe as opposed to the intricacies of the American electoral college system or the environmental ethics around the use of wood burners. Since we had last been out properly, just the two of us (Vue – Eddie Redmayne – lots of yawning), we'd become joint CEOs of a brand-new person. Why should we feel embarrassed about having a post-match analysis of this gargantuan life shift?

Parents should never feel ashamed if their conversation is dominated by reflections on the life they are shaping or discussions about how that life has really turned a corner with carrots recently. (As long as no one else is there, of course. Don't be that boring bastard who ruins dinner parties with tales of little Ewan's dairy allergy. Nothing kills a vibe quicker than an explanation of the milk ladder.)

And so, on our first night away from our girl, that is exactly what we did. We spoke about our Ratbag. We talked about the last few months, experienced together, but so often very separately. We chatted about how dreadful it had been but how sweet it could sometimes be too. We spoke about our relationship, what we were doing well, what we could do better, all the while in strong, unified agreement that Prosecco is very good. We scoffed a pizza, helped ourselves to some free samples of Mr Pretzel and were home in bed by 10.00 pm.

Tiddly and rejuvenated, I fell asleep knowing that the old me had staged a comeback, even just for a few hours. Sassy. Silly. A strong female lead in my own life *slow-mo hair toss while wearing trouser suit*. It would be a while before she was a regular cast member, but I had enjoyed seeing this surprise cameo.

Phil and I now try to go on regular date nights. Babies will unite you in a way you've never known before, as you stare amazed, revelling in their tiny achievements that the rest of the world will find as engaging as a piece of MDF. But babies can also drive you apart, quickly and easily, as you fight for space, time and appreciation. The baby books tell you how often your contractions should be before you call the hospital and how much sleep a 17-week-old should be getting, but I have yet to read a section in any of these guides entitled: 'Mourning Your Old Marriage' – a chapter in which the author tells you how the inevitable pressure a child can place on a relationship can push you so far apart it becomes possible to miss your partner when you are both in the same room.

I can be a very kind and thoughtful wife, but unfortunately, I also have zero grace, limited empathy and harbour grudges like Arya Stark in *Game of Thrones*. Add to the mix some perennial parental tiredness and a stressful, unpredictable job, and WELCOME TO THE ANGRY WIFE CLUB! Come on in! The water's tepid and no, you can't go to the gym tomorrow, because I want to organise the towels and you had half an hour to yourself on Tuesday when you did the recycling. And this is why date night is key – getting out of the house just the two of us is crucial in helping me remember that there is, in fact, more to marriage than adding to the never-ending 'List of Resentments' that I harbour in my brain.

As much as I hate the terminology ('date night' sounds like something a shunned 1950s housewife would implement with an indifferent adulterous husband) if you want to keep sight of who you both once were and who, one day, you'll have space to be again, then book one in. I tend to be the 'date night' organiser in our house – blocking out some time, booking a babysitter and telling Phil to inform his lover he's busy that evening. These nights start at 5.00 pm to ensure we're home by 10.00 pm, because, while I'm extremely fun, going to sleep drunk at midnight and then being awoken by a small person at 5.00 am to watch a looped YouTube video of 'Wheels on the shitting Bus' is a level of desperation I have no desire to experience (again). These date nights always involve food and booze, with the occasional foray into 'a fun planned activity', the most recent one being a session at a VR gaming room. Yes. A VR gaming room where Phil and I spent 60 thrilling minutes in 3D headsets shooting orcs with bows and arrows. Was it a romantic date or a 12-year-old boy's birthday party? We'll never truly know. But as the saying goes, 'The couple that murders pixelated fantastical creatures together, stays together'.

There is, of course, a huge elephant in the (VR gaming) room I haven't yet addressed in regard to date nights which is, if done right, the fact that you will be leaving your house while your child remains there. Gulp. And so comes a really big first, the biggest first there is – the 'first time you leave your baby'.

★

My first dabble with some child-free action was when my babe was about three weeks old. I declared I wanted/needed 30 minutes shore leave, so I left the baby with my husband and used my precious time to walk to Lidl to parade down the middle aisle (mindfulness comes in many forms). For me, this separation from my child felt absolutely doable and, if anything, really rather nice. Ratbag was safe with someone who loved her, and I was able to check out some great deals on sheepskin-lined crocs and waffle makers. No one was traumatised. No one missed anyone. Everyone was a winner. Everyone got waffles.

The next level up in the Separation Game is likely to be the: 'first time you leave the baby with an extended family member'. For me, it was when my daughter was a month old – my mum came over for some one-on-one Ratbag action while Phil and I grabbed a cuppa at a nearby café (the place where the barista is on first name terms with my boobs). It all went well, we were home within an hour with my still sleeping baby none the wiser, and I'd only texted my mum 400 times. Hurrah! Waffles all round!

If you're lucky enough to have a willing mama or mama-in-law in your lives, please take her up on any offers of babysitting she throws out. She will adore the chance to swoop in for some top-notch Grandma-ing, and you get to switch off your mother's danger radar that leaves you in a constant and exhausting process of risk assessment. Although, I would say, even with close family it's a good idea to discuss some childcare ground rules before you leave the house – something a friend of mine came to realise a little too late after she left her four-month-old with her mum to go to a fancy awards event.

A couple of hours after my friend arrived at the bash, she received a frantic call from Granny saying that the babe was going bananas, and she couldn't settle him. My friend raced back home to find a screaming baby and a grandmother so out of ideas that, at one point, she revealed she'd attempted to soothe her grandson by (brace yourself) 'breastfeeding' him. Needless to say, the child was deeply unimpressed. Poor lad – it must have been like being offered an empty pint glass on a roasting summer's day. Imagine his reaction when he's older and finds out – 'Was I close to Granny when I was growing up?' . . . 'Well, you could say that, son.'

Breastfeeding grandmothers aside, it felt to me that leaving my baby wasn't half as emotionally taxing as I thought it might be. That was until I bumped up against the other childcare option – the far more daunting: 'first time you leave your child with a stranger'. Now, some parents won't have to cross this bridge for years if they have a willing and available local support network, but for me, not living close to my family and also being saddled with stupid work commitments meant that at about three months, I decided to start using a babysitting app. I would hire someone to sit with my child downstairs in my house while I wrote upstairs. A taster session of true child abandonment.

I naturally spent a long time drawing up a short list of potential sitters before choosing my preferred candidate, in the end going for a lady who not only had excellent reviews but also had two children of her own and bore a striking resemblance to Susie Dent, the clever words lady from *Countdown*. I assumed that this meant she had both a good heart and a great grasp of grammar. A few days later, Fake Susie arrived at my home and quickly settled in well with my baby. I dashed upstairs, spent two hours writing, dashed back down and, finding everyone alive and well, immediately booked her in again for another day. When she left, I was frankly quite confused as to why people make such a fuss about leaving their kids with randoms. What was there to be upset about? My baby was happy being fed and bounced 20 feet away below me, while above her head, Mummy wrote jokes and perused the MailOnline 'ironically'. A great time had by all.

It was when, on the babysitter's fourth session with us and I suggested she take my baby for a walk around the park, that I began to realise that I may be slightly more attached to my daughter than I had first thought. I trusted Fake Susie, and yet, when she and my child failed to return after what I (arbitrarily) decided was the correct length of time for a park stroll, a flutter of fear started to rise in me. I grabbed my phone and messaged her with a series of texts that were cheerful but with a strong subtext of 'WHERE THE SHIT ARE YOU?':

First up: 'Hiya! 👋 Just checking in to see if she's being a good girl?'

Two minutes later: 'Me again! You've been ages! 😵 All OK? When do you think you'll be back?'

Two minutes later: 'Hi – sorry to be annoying but can you message me? I'm being a neurotic mother aren't I, LOL! Thank you – sorry! Haha. Sorry! 😂😂😂😂😂😂😂 (Please message me ASAP).'

No reply.

It was at that point I decided that the simplest explanation for their failure to return was due to the fact that Fake Susie had stolen my baby. The two of them were most likely on their way to an airport right now, about to start a new life together in Peru on an alpaca farm. I grabbed my phone again and opened the babysitting app, certain that I would now find the babysitter's profile and all her details deleted like the classic disappearing child-stealer she was. Oh. Her profile was still there, along with the 300 five-star ratings she'd been given. Hmmm. 'Well . . . so what?!' I irrationally rationalised, 'Just because she's still on the app doesn't mean anything. She's still probably a baby-stealer, but just one who's very bad at staying on top of crime admin.'

Another two minutes passed. Just as I was about to call the number on the app's contact page to ask to be put through to the Child Robbery Department, there was a knock at the front door. You'll never guess who it was. I ran downstairs, my body pumping with enough adrenalin to allow me to pull the moon from the sky if I'd have wanted. There they were, the baby cooing in the buggy and nice, kind Fake Susie, still very nice and kind, and also very apologetic to have missed my messages – they'd been distracted having a nice sing-song. A NICE SING-SONG. I laughed too hard and said not to worry. Nonetheless, it definitely felt a little 'off' letting my child out of my sight in the care of someone I didn't know the bones of. 'But what else can I do?' I would say to myself, 'I have no option – this self-employed mama has to work. Waffle makers don't buy themselves.'

And so we come to the tricky old world of parental leave and the return to work . . . strap on in. Or, preferably, let's all just move to Sweden.

12

Work 2

It seems sensible at the beginning of a chapter about parents going back to work to flag that obviously not everyone will return to their old job. Some people will choose to stay at home after they've had a baby and others are strong-armed into it due to the prohibitive cost of childcare – which can, in some cases, eat up an entire wage and more. In this section I'll inevitably be banging the drum for the plight of working parents, but let me just say that to anyone who chooses or is forced via circumstance to stay at home with their children full-time, I am under no illusion that you live a life of unending laughter and fun-packed days. Being a stay-at-home parent is both a full-on and full-time position, with the added benefit of having zero benefits and an hourly rate of nothing. Yes, the commute is minimal, yes, there'll be occasional opportunities to sip lukewarm tea in front of *This Morning* for approximately three minutes before you have to deal with a felt tip emergency, and yes, at the end of the year, you may have a tax bill of zero, but this vital, invisible job is incredibly bloody taxing. So this is me, standing tall to salute all of you stay-at-homers. Hear that? It's the 21-gun salute I've organised in your honour ringing out over the soft play centre as you look at your watch and try to work out how you will fill the rest of the 67 hours left in this day. But for now, it's time to jump into the space I inhabit – a land of mums and dads attempting to bring up a child while simultaneously bringing home the bacon. And it all starts with parental leave.

Most employed women are entitled to 52 weeks of Statutory Maternity Leave, but not all those mothers will be eligible to be *paid* for that time, and even if you are fortunate enough to receive pay, only 39 out of the 52 weeks *has* to be paid. Still with me? No? Fair enough. Maternity packages vary enormously from the very brilliant (hat tip to the companies who offer 36 weeks' maternity leave at full salary) to the pitiful basic legal requirement (six weeks' paid leave at 90% of your wage and the remaining 33 weeks paid at around £151 per week). Regardless of how substantial a woman's maternity leave package starts out, by the end of it the majority of women find their payments have decreased dramatically or simply stopped completely.

And then, of course, there's the world I lurk within. While I may work in the entertainment industry I am, to all intents and purposes, just another freelancer, small business owner or self-employed new mum who may, if she ticks the right boxes, qualify for Maternity Allowance of around £151 per week for 39 weeks. Now, if we assume parenting a small baby during that time frame is a 24/7 job, then over that 39-week period a woman on that statutory pay is earning around £1.11 an hour. Even if we give her eight hours off a night to sleep, (HAHAHAHAHA, that is the best joke I have ever written) her hourly rate only goes up to around £1.34, while the living wage in the UK is around £10. Oh. Perhaps we are meant to invoice for that shortfall? Or maybe we just wait for a knock on the door during our kid's first birthday from a man in a red jacket, People's Postcode Lottery-style? I am still waiting for my top-up, presumably down to some sort of clerical error, but I'm sure any day now I'll receive an apology card from the Department of Work and Pensions with a few pound coins sellotaped inside.

While it's true that having children is a choice, let's not forget that those same children will one day be working adults paying into the system. The government is not doing a mother a favour by chucking £1.11 per hour into her cap, the mother is doing the *government* a favour by raising someone who will one day potentially care for the elderly, or perhaps work in the NHS, teach in schools or end up paying 45% income tax. Children are not luxury items; children are necessary to the functioning of our future society.

The good news in all this is that at least it's not just new mothers who are treated badly; it's new fathers too! Hurrah! A triumph for equality! Paternity leave is arguably even more of a shitshow than maternity leave. (Fun fact: if you are a female partner in a same-sex relationship, your leave will still be referred to as paternity leave *slow hand clap*). If they qualify in the first place (and not all will), fathers/partners can look forward to two weeks of statutory pay at around £151 per week, and then they are straight back to it. Some partners won't be able to afford to take that two-week pay cut, meaning they may have to return to work sooner, or in some cases, take no leave at all. Both of those options seem unthinkable to me.

My husband was fortunate in that his two weeks' paternal leave was offered at full pay, and he then topped that up with three weeks' stockpiled annual leave – and thank god for that. Him returning to work when my child was two weeks' old remains unimaginable to me – at this point, I was still walking like a lame velociraptor and doing lots of secret shower crying. I was certainly in no fit state, mentally or physically, to fly solo. And, as is the case for many couples, what if you have other children? A school-aged child requiring drop-offs and picks-ups, hot dinners and homework help, or perhaps a tantrum-ing toddler, or perhaps both, or *more*, and it seems inconceivable that a woman should be left alone this soon. (As I write this, I am thinking of single parents who face this issue and so many more from the very outset. I see you, and you are astonishing.)

Thankfully, there are some happily notable exceptions with big names like Etsy and Aviva offering gender blind 'parental leave' as opposed to maternal/paternal, which see both new mothers *and* new fathers entitled to 26 weeks fully paid leave. This is what we need. Without better paternal leave, childcare, in the vast majority of cases, becomes the default responsibility of mothers, which in turn leads to an enforced career break, whether it's wanted or not. Without better paternal leave, hiring a woman continues to be seen as the 'riskier' choice by employers because it's only women who can disappear for a year to raise a child. Without better paternal leave, the gender pay gap is perpetuated, and our little girls hurtle straight towards the same glass ceiling that their mothers and grand-mothers have already bashed up against time and again.

Some of you may now be thinking, 'Woah woah woah there, Ellie, what about the UK's Shared Parental Leave policy the government rolled out so proudly a few years ago? The exciting scheme that allows both parents to share up to 50 weeks of leave and 37 weeks' pay? That's basically what you're after, isn't it, you big, greedy time-off-loving wench?' Well, in a way, absolutely yes, so much so that later on, my husband and I utilised this exact policy which allowed him to take three precious months off, starting when Ratbag was nine months old. We felt incredibly lucky he had this opportunity to be her primary carer. And yet . . . well, where do I begin?

First up, there are a few major flaws with the policy, starting with the narrow eligibility parameters that mean agency workers and people on zero-hour contracts are immediately disqualified from utilising the scheme. Boom. It's now only an option for three in seven families.

Then there's the fact that even for the eligible, it's a complicated, rarely utilised policy. When I started to explore the scheme, I soon found that our combined employment situation was far too niche to be able to source any online advice. In the end, I had to consult an employment lawyer to help work out if we could even use the bloody policy in the first place. Not the most accessible start.

And that isn't the worst of it. The real kicker is the fact that unless enhanced by an employer, partners are only offered the statutory £151 per week for the duration of their leave. For many families, the simple maths of living means Shared Parental Leave is an immediate no-go, which explains why only a pitiful 1% of people eligible for the scheme have actually used it.

There is no doubt that, compared to many other people, as a couple we are fortunate in our financial situation, but just like everyone, we have cut our cloth according to our usual income. To suddenly forfeit Phil's wage was certainly not something we undertook lightly, and it's the reason he only took three months and not longer. I have no doubt that many partners would love to have this opportunity to spend time with their child, to share the burden and to get a temporary reprieve from the cycle of only seeing their baby for a few hours a day; however, until it is financially viable, this scheme is virtually meaningless.

In reality, I only took around three months' maternity leave, which I know sounds quite short. It's key to reiterate here that my job is a funny old fish. For me, returning from maternity leave was nowhere near as full-on as a returning mother diving back into a 40-hour week in an office, or long shifts on her feet in a hair salon or shop. I could ease my way back into things with a few carefully selected bits, thanks to a combination of my husband, my mum and Fake Susie providing childcare. The flexibility in my job allows me to pick and choose what I do, depending on whether the project looks fun and/or will pay for a new Rixo dress. But the price of this flexibility, ironically, was that no one was paying me to be off in the first place and, more importantly (or as it felt at the time), a fear loomed large that if I didn't get back in the game quickly I would have no career to return to. The biggest problem in all this was that stupid-smug-pregnant-Ellie had papered crying-struggling-new-mum-Ellie into a really crappy corner with some decision-making best described as cavalier.

When I was eight-and-a-half months pregnant, I announced that I would be doing a new stand-up tour the following summer. The marketing images were published, and the tickets went on sale all before I'd even met the child the show would inevitably be about. Clueless-pregnant-me thought that a tour sounded like something fun to aim for, 'a nice little project' to keep me ticking over while I was bored at home twiddling my thumbs with all that free time I was going to have. 'Writing a new show with a newborn baby? That sounds pretty manageable,' I had thought. 'I'm sure NCT Janet would have given me a heads up if she thought committing to huge work obligations in the first year of your child's life was a bad idea. Let's do this! What can possibly go wrong?!'

Cut to a tableau of me three months after my daughter was born, sitting in my ever-present red dressing gown feeding my baby, staring at my seventh episode of *Undercover Boss America* of the morning, and experiencing a continuous cycle of thoughts that all distilled down to the singular sentiment of, 'FUCK.'

My brain was slurry. I had no opinions, I had no creativity, I had no ideas. I was human mundanity. I was the physical incarnation of Sunday afternoons spent watching *Antiques Roadshow*. To suddenly put myself in a position where I had to generate jokes when I felt unfunny on an almost elemental level was an impossible pressure. It was now March, and the tour was due to begin in August. I cried on my sister, saying it was a hopeless task. With her trademark bluntness, she said, 'Well, just cancel it then. Who cares? You're not exactly Michael Jackson.' Quite right. She's always been highly skilled at simultaneously making me laugh while clubbing my ego into submission. I knew she was right, and yet I still stupidly soldiered on with it all, too proud to say I wasn't coping so well, concerned about the ramifications for my career if I did otherwise.

I did find, though, that not all work is equal. While the long-term responsibility of the tour hung over me, huge and heavy, I did other jobs when my babe was small, which raised and cheered me. The pressure of writing a new show was draining – hope trickled out of me like syrup from a tapped maple tree, but I found that projects I could dip in and out of energised my new strange body, topping it up with purpose. And the sillier, the better.

My equivalent of the 'first full day back in the office' was suitably ridiculous – filming an episode of *The Crystal Maze* alongside Gemma Collins and Arg from *TOWIE*, as well as, you guessed it, only my BFF Carol bloody Vorderman. (I can confirm that Carol's two-time 'Rear of the Year' filled out her boiler suit sensationally, like a mathematical Kardashian.)

The show filmed in Bristol, so Phil took a day off work, and I left him with our tiny daughter and her accompanying instruction manual, which was similar in length to *Wolf Hall*. I'd even written a secret message at the bottom of the document (yes, I'd typed it up and printed it out) to check that Phil had read the whole thing. I would later quiz him on the secret message. Reader, he had not read the whole thing.

I took an early train from Paddington and thoroughly enjoyed having a croissant and a tea in peace (aside from my big noisy breast pump that was syphoning off my wares so my tits wouldn't explode in the Aztec zone).

Much like my willingness to breastfeed in public, I was also strangely unfazed by expressing milk in public, so there I sat in my seat, pumping away. Certainly a good way to ensure you get a table of four to yourself. I think my probably unusual blasé mindset came down to a combination of laziness and that same stubbornness again – yes, I suppose I *could* go and find a discreet toilet to sit in to do it, but:

1) Why should I?

2) I like looking at sheep out of the window.

3) Why should I?

So there I sat, multi-tasking, posting a few 'pumping my bristols on the way to Bristol' Instagram stories, which in itself made the journey seem worthwhile.

When I arrived at the studio, I squeezed my still foreign post-partum flesh into a *Crystal Maze* boilersuit. While Carol had the backside in the bag, my wobbly stomach certainly gave me edge around the front, thanks to some impressive straining camel toe action.

The day was perfectly absurd, and it felt wonderful to do my job again. As is often the case, filming began to run over schedule, and I became worried about missing Ratbag's final feed at 10.00 pm, which I'd promised Phil I'd be home in time to do myself. The production team were very sweet, and we powered through, but as time ticked towards my train's departure it was clear I was going to have to race to get it. In the end, the producers whisked me out of the building and bundled me into a car towards the station like I was the Prime Minister escaping sniper fire. I made the train by about ten seconds and collapsed into a seat panting, only then realising that I was still wearing the show's boiler suit. Fortunately, it was far more breastfeeding-friendly than I imagine the garment's designer had ever intended, so I spent the journey home knocking back Smiths Scampi Fries and pump-pumping it up. Once home, I galloped upstairs to my girl. As she fed sleepily in the dark, I felt the Perspex crystal in my pocket that a producer had shoved in my hand as he frog-marched me towards my getaway car. A proper little memento of my first day back in the office, a trophy that I have decided *all* new mums should receive on their first day back – whether they've pushed Gemma Collins through a pipe in the Industrial zone or not.

Around this time, my parents-in-law flew in from Sydney to meet their granddaughter and were staying with us, meaning that now we essentially had two live-in 70-year-old au pairs. Coincidentally, their stay lined up with my first job abroad, which would mean me staying away for a few nights. Leaving for this trip and knowing that Ratbag was in the care of my husband as well as his folks made it all seem much more doable. I knew that while I was gone, like a tiny empress, she would have three adults at her beck and call. That is the person/servant ratio an oligarch would be proud of.

My trip away also provided a great chance for my mother-in-law to have unbridled access to her granddaughter without me stalking around trying to assert my alpha matriarch credentials. A daughter-in-law/mother-in-law relationship can be a tricky beast to navigate at the best of times but especially when there is a new grandchild involved. In truth, I am not proud of how I acted towards my M.I.L during her stay. Finding your feet as a new mum is incredibly hard, and even harder when you have a live-in audience. Through no malice on her part (she is a wonderful lady and a doting grandmother), my insecurities allowed her mere presence to make me feel like I was being permanently observed by Ofsted.

The work trip in question was memorable not just for it being my first proper escape but also because I used it to test run a sweet new piece of kit. I'd been given a cordless USB-charged breast pump, which you can just shove in your bra – no wires or hands needed, all run by an app. An APP. This was revolutionary. There I was, sitting in a restaurant in the departure lounge at Heathrow, chowing down on some eggs Benedict (hollandaise on the side, thanks) while at the same time effortlessly expressing milk into the little container nestled in my DD cup. This was fantastic. My boobs were going to stay mastitis-free, and I was certain I'd be able to maintain a good supply of Mama's Nesquik until I returned to my child.

My flight was called; I paid my bill and headed towards the plane. As I stood on the shuttle taking me to the gate, I noticed a group of teenage boys at the other end of the train looking at me. At first, I thought I'd imagined it, but no. They were definitely looking. *Admiring* even. 'Well, I know my eyebrows are having a good day, but I must have snapped back even more than I'd realised! Still got it, Tayls, still got it,' I thought proudly.

It was only when I arrived at the gate that I thought to check the pump that was still beavering away in my bra. I looked down. Oh god. So silent and discreet, it turned out the pump had been, if anything, too effective – my cup had runneth over. My left boob had filled the pump's bottle totally, and with nowhere else for liquid to be stored, without me realising, milk had been pouring down my now soaked top. Those boys on the train were not looking at me with desire, those boys were looking at me and thinking that the strange lady who kept winking at them had ruined wet T-shirt competitions forever.

So there I was, sodden, creamy, and now faced with the team of people I'd be working with for the next few days who were all booked on the same flight. Talk about first impressions. I greeted them shiftily, attempting to cover my wet bits by draping the scarf I was wearing vertically down my body, like a distinguished woman in her 70s collecting an MBE. By the time the plane landed, my T-shirt was a crusty, cheesy plank.

My breasts became the emblem of that trip. I was filming with an all-male crew who had been told I would need regular breaks every few hours to express milk. The deal was that, at every location, they would pre-arrange a secluded spot for me to do this in private. It turned out that the secluded spots they'd helpfully arranged included a table in the middle of a tapas bar and a desk in a functioning open-plan office. Not ideal, and certainly not the most relaxing times in the day. Whenever it became time for one of 'Ellie's special breaks', a producer would come up to me looking ashen and say, 'Right . . . you go and err . . . *swallows nervously* do what you . . . *cough* need to do,' as if every four hours I was nipping off to dispose of a body.

Even as I boarded the plane on the journey home, my diva boobs had their eyes (nips) set on yet more limelight. I was sitting in a row of three seats: me on the aisle, a vacant seat in the middle and a man in a suit next to the window. The man was about my age, and smiled a twinkly smile as I sat down. Once we were airborne, I reached into my bag and produced my huge breast pump (the little in-bra one had not survived the flood damage of the outbound disaster) and placed it on the tray table in front of me. Clearly having no idea what the strange object was, the flirty man, sensing an opportunity, nodded to the pump and quipped, 'Old school MP3 player is it?' Undoubtedly, an absolute zinger. If I wasn't a married, lactating woman, I'm sure we'd be mini-breaking in Prague together right now. I laughed heartily, partly at what he'd said, but mostly because I knew what was to come.

I started getting sorted, untangling wires and screwing on lids before discreetly hooking up my udders, the whole time while my beau stole glances at his enigmatic love, who appeared to be ferreting around in very strange places. And then came the big switching on. I hit the button, and the pump noise kicked in: 'HUHHHHHHHHH . . . HUHHHHHHHHH . . . HUHHHHHHHH'. Within a few seconds, Suit Man clearly clocked onto what was happening because two things occurred in quick succession. Firstly, his penis shrivelled up and died (this is speculative, but by the look on his face, I think likely to be accurate). Secondly, he pulled the duty-free brochure out of the pocket in front of him, which he then went on to study intently for the remainder of the journey, either determined to find a great deal on Joop! *or* using it as a physical blinker to block out the milky horror show happening next door. There were no more suggestive smiles or funny quips. Sigh. Another great love story quashed before it had even begun.

Aside from all the boob-based awkwardness that rumbled on throughout the trip, I had really enjoyed the time away. I'd worked long days and missed my daughter, but my husband made sure to send plenty of proof-of-life pictures, plus I had access to limitless room service and slept for eight hours a night, so, swings and roundabouts. I would go on a few more trips in those first 12 months of my daughter's life, the longest stint being for nearly two weeks. In all honesty, I found these trips as restorative as much as they were hard work. They filled my tank with energy and enthusiasm, meaning that when I parachuted back into being 'mum', I found I was able to wind the absolute bejesus out of that bobbin better than ever. But things undoubtedly became harder when Phil's stint of Shared Parental Leave ended when Ratbag turned one. For the first time, there was no parent or grandparent at home solely on baby duty. Whether we liked it or not, it was time to jump into the world of formalised childcare.

The four options for paid childcare are: childminder, au pair, nursery or nanny. All solid options, all bloody expensive. The average cost for a full-time nursery place for a child under two in the UK is £252 a week or edging close to £13,000 per year (more if you live in London). If you opt for a live-out nanny, it's a staggering £500–800 per week (again, more if you live in London). Compare that to the family utopia of Sweden, where every child is guaranteed a spot at a public preschool where charges are capped at around £100 per month. Man, I love those tall blonde bastards.

Childcare costs in the UK are some of the most expensive in the world for a variety of reasons, including lack of government funding and also the legal specifications around adult to children ratios. In the UK, one nursery worker must be present for every four children aged two to three, whereas in France that ratio is one adult to eight kids, who are presumably so often left to their own devices, they can usually be found smoking skinny cigarettes and reading Proust. Regardless of the reasons *why* parents in the UK face such a hefty monthly bill, quite simply, these prices mean that formal childcare is not an option for some families and arguably barely sustainable for many others. I remember my sister telling me about a period when both her kids were in nursery; after paying fees and her travel she was taking home around £70 a month. £70 for a month of wrangling a baby, a toddler, a commute and a 'part-time' role that inevitably spilled over into her days off. Like many returning mothers, she felt this is what she had to do in order to keep a seat at the table, scared that if she left, that seat would be whipped away as the game of 'career progression musical chairs' proceeded without her. For solo parents without a second wage to rely on, childcare costs can be even more devastating, with these fees eating up an average 67% of a single parent's income.

Before I had my daughter, I was told by some local parents that if I wanted to secure a spot at one of the neighbourhood's good nurseries and not one of the places that was essentially a primary colour-painted gulag, I should really have started putting my name on waiting lists shortly before I sat my GCSEs. Trying to make up for lost time, I began to look at places for my unborn child when I was seven months pregnant.

Just as my neighbours foretold, one of the nurseries I visited – a fancy hippy place which boasted an organic plant-based menu prepared by an ex-Ottolenghi chef – told me during a tour of the facility that, in all honesty, I was unlikely to ever get a space for this child, but if I went on to have a second one then I could transfer our place on the waiting list to that hypothetical baby instead. It's now nearly three years since I registered at that place, and I still am yet to hear from them. What a great day that will be when my daughter graduates from university in 2040, and I finally get a call to say that a spot is available in the Sunshine Room at Tiny Teeny Tots. In the end, we settled on a brand-new childcare centre that was big, bright and had cameras in every room, meaning I'd be able to watch Ratbag steal maracas from the mouths of other kids from the comfort of my own home.

The settling-in period was, I would say, pretty heartbreaking for everyone involved. All the parenting my husband and I had done up until that point was about making our daughter feel loved and safe. Nursery felt like the undoing of that. From being at home with one-on-one attention to shoving her in a room with strangers and a menagerie of other germ-riddled screaming infants. Her little face, when I would come and collect her, was a snapshot of anguish as if I'd left her with a pack of hyenas as opposed to some nice ladies with childcare qualifications and exceptional Goosey Goosey Gander skills. She'd see me at the window of her room, her lip would quiver, tears streaming down her face with a look that said, '. . . What the FUCK, man?! Where have you BEEN? Are you insane? I am your BABY?? You can't just leave me! I thought you were my person! Who even *are* these people? Why are they trying to make me eat cauliflower? What *is* cauliflower? And where's the TV? Thank god I never have to come here ever again . . .' Day in, day out.

In the end, it took around six weeks to settle/break her in. I spent a lot of that time Googling variations of the words 'nursery' 'baby' and 'trauma'. I knew her going to childcare was necessary for us as a family, but it certainly didn't sit well. Friends would say, 'Mine didn't like it at the beginning either Ellie, it's really normal for them to be upset.' Yes, millions of people like me around the world put their small kids in daycare because we have no other choice but to any of us, do their tears of separation feel *normal*? From an evolutionary point of view, humans leaving vulnerable infants in strange locations with strange people is surely anything but normal? Aren't we basically meant to be like monkeys, carrying our babies on our backs as we swing together through the jungle until they are old enough to go it alone? But how could I? My jungle was one of meetings and late-night gigs – my baby monkey was far too noisy and sticky to survive here. So then did I need to *change* my jungle? Abandon work and hang out at kiddy gymnastics and the M&S café, lamenting the career I gave up for the sake of the little chimp? What was I doing all this for? What did I really want from life? And why have I dragged out this jungle metaphor so painfully?

But, as always, for all of us, it was 'just a phase'. Ratbag acclimatised, and so did I. Partly because time passed and partly because, essentially, we were out of options. I had to work, I wanted to work, and for that to happen, she needed to be somewhere I wasn't.

The first day I left my daughter at nursery and she *didn't* cry gave me a sense of elation that I imagine football fans experience when their team wins and they push over a tram to celebrate. I was *beside* myself. I couldn't believe what I'd just witnessed – she had waved goodbye and then just walked in. *Just walked in.* That was it. Where was the quivering chin? Where were the wails of torment? Where were the pangs of guilt deep within my shattered soul? I rang my husband, 'Darling! She didn't cry! She must have forgiven us! She must like it!' I shrieked euphorically. 'Great news!' he said, 'She's finally learnt to internalise her unhappiness like the rest of us!'

I bloody love nursery now. I am a dirty convert. Trauma? WHAT TRAUMA? Nursery means I can sit in a café or go for a run or go to a meeting or do some writing or record something silly or do anything I bloody well want because I DON'T HAVE TO LOOK AFTER MY OWN CHILD. What's she having for lunch? DON'T KNOW, DON'T CARE, NOT MY RESPONSIBILITY. Oh no, she's weed through her tights, has she? NOT MY ISSUE, WHACK HER IN SOME TROUSERS FISHED OUT FROM THE BIN OF SHAME. I genuinely can't think of many other things in my entire life that have lifted my spirits in the way nursery has, aside perhaps for the Paris filter on Instagram.

My daughter trots in every day as happy as Larry (Larry is a notorious early years education lover). The place is colourful and chaotic, full of lefty parents keen to sign permission slips for their child to partake in activities like yoga and Mandarin classes. And just to be clear, they are not lazy punchlines I have just plopped in. Yoga and Mandarin are genuinely some of the weekly activities undertaken by my tiny daughter. She is apparently a natural in her Mandarin sessions – according to her daily record sheet, she has learnt how to say the Chinese for 'coconut' and 'pineapple', which will really help the next time me and her pop to Beijing to get shitfaced on pina coladas.

My delight when I leave her at nursery and walk away humming George Michael's 'Freedom' as I cross the road without having to wait for the green man, is only bettered by the delight I experience when I pick her up again at the end of the day. She belts towards me, smelling of another woman's perfume, excited to tell me how she's been to the park or made a snowman or 'done Baby Shark' as if it's a verb. (90% of the time, she will have done none of these things, but, like many pathological liars, she's extremely charismatic.)

Even at the worst of my initial nursery anxiety, I have always tried to bat away the temptation to be drawn into the 'mum guilt', narrative that I despise. It's either un-gendered 'parental guilt' or it can sod off. It is not for mothers alone to navigate the burden of a work/child balance. If you, like me, ever feel a sneak of self-reproach edge in, I urge you to try and tough-love yourself out of it. Remind your brain, as utilitarian as it sounds, that each of us has a role to play in a family, even our children. For my husband and 1, our job is to work and pay bills, and for Ratbag, her job is to go to nursery, and bloody well do Baby Shark. Women should not feel bad about having time apart from their children and having the audacity to enjoy it. When my child is at nursery, I end the day knowing I have worked hard, and she has done 20 activities she would never get to do at home. I don't spend our time away from one another in lovelorn misery, but rather I end the day with a bubbly Christmas Eve sense of excitement as I go to collect her. Sometimes I think I love her the most when I'm not with her. I have come to realise that I'm a better mother when I don't have to mother all the time.

When I do see my daughter again, and she runs towards me with a beaming gappy smile yelling, 'Mama's here! It's Mama!' knocking me backwards with a hurricane of happiness, I think she understands that even though Mummy sometimes goes away, Mummy always comes back.

13

Destruction

Having a kid creates change. Some of it will be good change, like getting out of having to go to that boring lunch or hen do because you now have the ultimate excuse up your sleeve: 'childcare issues'. (The phrase 'childcare issues' is a magic spell that wipes your diary clean from all those awful social engagements that mean you have to wash and go somewhere which isn't your sofa.) And best of all, unlike the death of a fictitious grandparent, there is no limit to how many times you can use it. Much like Jennifer Aniston, it never gets old.

However, while there is no doubt that blaming an imaginary flakey babysitter for having to cancel dinner with your flat-earther Uncle Gary is a joyous benefit to having a kid; I'm afraid to say there are many other child-enforced changes that bring far less sparkly outcomes. It's safe to say that having a child destroys your life and ruins everything that you previously enjoyed, for example . . .

Your House

The 'stuff' sneaks up on you. It begins deceptively slowly – a harmless if garish playmat appears in front of the sofa. 'That's ok,' you think, 'It's just one item. In fact, it's a nice hint of 'child' in a room that otherwise screams 'functional living space for two adults who like watching *The West Wing*'. Before long, though, the playmat will be joined by some cuddly toys which beget some books which will breed a baby bouncer, and then before you know it, you are surrounded by a one-metre-tall singing robot with an LED head, a fluffy twerking llama, and two shipping containers of Duplo. Everywhere, STUFF. By the time your kid is a toddler, your living room will be crammed with a mass of plastic detritus/future landfill, as well as one or two obligatory wooden items bought by child-free friends who naively think a timber abacus in muted pastels could ever compete with a neon marble-run that rewards the player with a loud fart noise as a finale.

And don't be fooled into thinking the problem is the size of your home. In the same way in olden times a terrapin was thought to grow to fit the size of the pond it inhabits, based on my scientific research, a child's crap will automatically increase to fill whatever place in which it resides, regardless of whether that is a one-bed flat or a mansion. At this very second, The Duchess of Cambridge is probably wandering around Kensington Palace tripping over trays of kinetic sand and Happy Meal toys, yelling, 'Charlotte, if you don't put away your Spirograph I'll take away your iPad AND your hereditary entitlement to the entire county of Norfolk!'

Children are like squatters; they have no respect for your property and, from a legal perspective, it is very hard to evict them. I already dream of the day when my daughter only wants to sulk in her room and the siege on my living room is ended. Never again will I need to worry about anyone colouring in the sofa with a Sharpie or seeing if my new spherical vase is, in fact, a 'bouncy ball'. The room will be neat, bare and peaceful, without cracker crumbs or Paw Patrol stickers stuck to the bottom third of the walls. And when that happens, I assume I'll go up into the loft, fish out the dancing llama, clutch it's twerking body against my chest and sob as I reminisce about the dreadful magical years when my feet were never safe from an unseen plastic Minion.

Weekends

Unless you're a weekend worker, the demise of a lazy Saturday morning is up there with the biggest losses any first-time parent has to face. Once you have a baby, you can kiss goodbye to lay-ins, late brunches and afternoons in the pub in favour of 6.00 am starts, Weetabix by 7.00 am and being in the playground by 8.00 am watching your child patrol the swings like a nightclub bouncer pushing away other toddlers while screaming, 'NO! MINE!' in their faces. At least once a month, my husband and I try to work out how we managed to while away all those kid-free weekends. What did we do with all those available hours? Aside from sleep, shag and eat shakshuka? What were the other hours filled with? Did we appreciate them?

I would like to create a parent's version of *Babestation* – a channel where knackered mums and dads tune in to watch non-parents read the weekend supplements as French café-style music gently tinkles in the background. There they would be on the screen, well-rested people who have showered, drinking piping hot tea from mugs they place dangerously close to the edge of very low tables. These people have never heard of the *Octonauts* and wouldn't know a Stickle Brick if it fell into their perfect White Russian concocted in the overpriced bar they can still afford to frequent because they don't have to pay for school shoes or dancing llamas.

Just as John Lennon imagined a life with no possessions, I imagine a weekend without having to pause *Sunday Brunch* while I clean up another human's faeces.

Relaxing holidays

When my daughter was seven months old, we went on our first family holiday to an all-inclusive child-friendly hotel in Majorca. After a mercifully uneventful flight, we checked in at the reception desk, where a stern Spanish lady secured luminous orange bands around our wrists and pointed us towards the main entrance to the resort. We took our bags and the baby, and walked through the gates of hell into a scene of war-like chaos.

Children *everywhere*; screaming, running, dancing to deafeningly loud pop music pumped out from speakers on what looked like Glastonbury's Pyramid Stage, where a flossing competition was getting under way. Whichever way you looked, there were sweaty, noisy people, some lying on messy sunbeds, some splashing like farmed salmon in rammed swimming pools, some in Speedos queuing for buffet restaurants where kids helped themselves to overflowing bowls of self-serve ice cream. Phil and I said nothing as we took in the scene of devastation before us. We were used to fancy mini-breaks in spa hotels in Wiltshire, or weeks spent reading quietly on the shores of a Greek Island, and now look where we were – drinking Sprite from plastic glasses as a nine-year-old Italian boy is crowned the Floss King and rewarded with a Maxibon sandwich. Christ alive. Had it really come to this?

Spending our precious time off in some kind of dystopian zoo where 1000 children with inflatable unicorns get off their tits on unlimited Fanta? I said a prayer for our old life and wished it well.

Kill me. Kill me now.

Fast forward to day three of the holiday, however, and it's safe to say that the Stockholm syndrome had well and truly kicked in. Love and hate are so similar in their intensity that it hadn't taken much to push me towards something approaching all-inclusive euphoria. This place was AWESOME! If I wasn't doing spin classes with my favourite club rep Gabriella, I was playing pétanque or taking the baby to watch her father play in violent water polo matches – where the losers were made to line up on the side of the pool and belly flop back in while a baying crowd pumped up on free-flowing San Miguel, cheered them on.

There was even a resort 'anthem' with accompanying dance routine, which I practised intensely. By the end of our stay, as soon as I heard the opening notes of the song, I would grab my daughter, sprint to the stage, barging past any other guest who dare block my path all so I could secure a spot next to my darling Gabriella, and revel in her orbit as we did the high-octane 'Volcano' side by side.

Everywhere we went in the hotel, there was a team of people being paid to cook food for us and then sweep up that food when my daughter chucked it on the floor. What restaurant should we go to for dinner? Italian? Seafood? Spanish? No, silly! The Tex-Mex, of course! They serve margaritas *and* have a nacho cheese fountain! Why would I ever go anywhere else?! I'm pleased to report that heaven really is a place on Earth, and it has limitless liquid Monterey Jack.

No, there weren't any hot stone massages, no, I didn't get to read any books and, yes, Phil did sprain his ankle during his final water polo match spelling an end to his budding 2028 Olympic ambitions, but we had so much good old fashioned *fun*. If you can't beat them, join them (for intermediate merengue.)

Your Ambition

In my old life, BC (Before Child), my aim was to move to America and become the next big thing, like a younger, female Hugh Grant with better teeth. I would live a jet-set lifestyle and become best friends with Kristen Wiig and end up replacing James Cordon as host of *The Late Late Show* after a sensational debut appearance on *SNL* that also prompts Sofia Coppola to call me 'the future of film'. An Academy Award nomination becomes inevitable, a win highly probable, a Hermes bag named after me, an absolute certainty. The world is my oyster. Anything is possible. I could aim for the highest high and stretch so far that I could almost touch it.

In my new life, TDSY (The Dry Shampoo Years), my main aim this week is to try and get Ratbag to eat a raspberry. Jarringly stereotypical, isn't it. Almost too on the nose. And yet here we are. Success has shape-shifted from the vast, the international, the stratospheric (with me at the centre of it all), to the small, the fundamental, the domestic – all rotating around a small child who loves pink wafer biscuits more than some members of her family.

That's not to say having a child totally erases a parent's personal sense of satisfaction and self-pride. I still want to work, win and succeed for my own fulfilment and also so I can earn money to buy important things like a university education for her and a brow lift for me. I still have lofty career ambitions, but those, and those of my husband, are now all viewed through the prism of how trying to achieve them would logistically impact our family. But perhaps this is just because our child is little. Perhaps when she's safely absorbed into the education system, our brains will have space to look outward, like many stay-at-home parents who jump back into work once their kids are in school and finally get some time back. But for now, while I am still more than happy to bask in the glow of any success of my own making, overshadowing that is the utter elation I feel when witnessing my daughter's tiny achievements.

She put the triangle-shaped block through the triangle-shaped hole? WHAT SWEET VICTORY IS THIS?!

She correctly made a 'twit twoo' noise after seeing a picture of an owl? READY THE RED ARROW FLY-PAST!

She drank a green smoothie packed full of fruit and veg because I told her it was magic pond water? INFORM ALL LOCAL PRESS OUTLETS OF THIS SPINACH-BASED MIRACLE.

You could argue that the reason some parents scale down their ambitions when they enter life with a child is because having a baby makes you inherently less selfish. This is the common narrative. The child-free are selfish, lazy and hedonistic, idling around in silk pyjamas on chaise longues while all the poor dog-tired parents dutifully repopulating the Earth scuttle between arse-wiping and making fish pie all on four hours' sleep and shots of Nespresso poured directly into the eyeball. Even as a parent, I don't buy this. I have always thought that having a baby, rather than being a selfless act, is arguably the most selfish thing a person can do. 'I adore me *so much* I'd like to make another tiny 'half me' that I can cuddle and kiss before introducing them to the back catalogue of 90s chanteuses, All Saints. Sure, I care about the environment, but not as much as I care about having a tiny human to dress up as a baby Morticia Addams for Halloween.'

Yes, having my daughter has made me less overtly self-obsessed, but I think that's largely due to me being so busy nurturing the piece of myself that is carried within *her*. Children are a physical manifestation of the ambition of their mothers and fathers. They *are* our hopes, our dreams and our promises. What I'm saying is, if my daughter doesn't win an Oscar by the time she's 18, I will expect a public-funded enquiry.

My body

My C-section scar lurks just below the top of my knickers, once a slash of Quality Street purple now faded to a patchy pink trail. My breasts are deflated, dragged down by the time they spent being a constantly-replenishing-vending-machine. My stomach is spongey and quivering, like a panna cotta that's been out of the fridge for too long. My body has decided that it's best if it keeps hold of some of the four stone I put on when pregnant, presumably for a rainy day. My old clothes don't fit in the same way. Some don't fit at all. There is more of me than there was.

For the first year after my daughter was born, I would look in the mirror and not understand what I saw there. That wasn't me. That was my head transplanted onto someone else's inflated body, swollen and wobbly with the ghost of a black line trailing down from an outie belly button that was trying to become an innie once more. This strange skin I inhabited shamed me. Sometimes it still does.

On my bad days, I go through a horrid ritual where I'll get out of bed, go into the bathroom for a wee and then stare in the mirror as I lift up my T-shirt to see how disappointing the body I've woken up in is today. Still not back to where I used to be? Sigh. I berate myself for having to bite the bullet and buy bigger sizes. Why is blubber spilling out and over my bra? Why do my old knickers, which used to be comfy and roomy, now leave red marks when I take them off?

I wonder why I haven't 'snapped back' like the women I see on Instagram, with 'before' shots of them heavily pregnant next to 'after' shots of them in a bikini looking like a tanned broom holding their six-week-old bundle of joy. As I mindlessly scroll on the sofa while my child watches *CBeebies*, I realise I haven't even had breakfast yet, and I'm already feeling like a pointless, sad old sow. Why don't I do five workouts a week? Why am I too lazy to weigh out my daily allowance of chicken sausages and protein powder? *Why have I failed?*

On my good days, though, I stare at myself and know that my body has given the ultimate sacrifice. Just like Bruce Willis in *Armageddon* when he gives up his own life in order to explode an asteroid heading towards Earth, my stomach selflessly relinquished all hope of ever appearing in a crop top again in order to create my Ratbag. How *dare* I think these horrible things about my perfectly imperfect flesh. My tummy housed her, my legs bore her weight, my dear old knockers silently and thanklessly fed my girl *life*.

I am the heaviest I have ever been; my thighs are like new lovers who must be in physical contact at all times, I house a colony of cellulite on my pancake-flat mum-bum, and I look utterly knackered because I *am* utterly knackered, and yet, even if I may forget it sometimes, I know what size pants I wear is the least interesting thing about me.

Pre-baby, my body was a show home – bright, aspirational and tastefully lit by stylish lamps from Heals. But then my baby moved in, and the walls got scuffed, the carpet got stained, and one of the lamps got broken during a game of indoor frisbee. The 'show home' became a 'home'. It's now very unlikely to feature on any Pinterest boards, but what it lacks in chic decor it makes up for in stories and heart. My body has incubated, born and nourished my favourite thing in the world, so the least I can do is cut the trash talk. Despite what our inner critics may tell us, not looking like we did when we were 19 is not, in fact, a crime we must spend the rest of our lives trying to atone for. To risk sounding like an inspirational fridge magnet, we all only get one go at living, so it's safe to say there is never *ever* time to waste crying in a New Look changing room because an 'XL' is a bit tight.

Your life

Becoming a parent by default heaves the remains of your old life into a skip, covers it in petrol and flicks in a lit cigarette. Kaboom. Everything is different. You are constantly tired both physically and mentally. Your brain is a personal Enigma machine, forever absorbing changing information and churning out possible responses – plans, times, childcare, what's for dinner, clothes to buy, school applications to research, costumes for World twatting Book Day (the first time our nursery declared they were celebrating this 'event' I explained that I hadn't had time to sort anything for my daughter, so she wouldn't be participating. Her key worker looked at me with pity and said, 'Don't worry – just dress her as a princess.' The next day we were greeted at the gates by a sea of Spidermen and Angelina Ballerinas with my daughter in jeans and a sweatshirt, as I claimed she was 1980s Princess Di visiting Alton Towers).

I am forever chastising myself about some new aspect of parenting I am failing at. What if I am not playing with my daughter enough or reading to her enough, teaching her enough, nourishing her enough, seeing her enough, leaving her enough, loving her enough, disciplining her enough? What if trying to be a good mother is making me a bad wife? Is it possible to do both properly? Do I have it within me to give enough to the person I chose as well as the person I made?

As a couple, having a child has forced us to re-evaluate everything we had previously thought set in cement. Our daughter has irrevocably changed our priorities, the little rat. We have left London and landed back in the Essex suburb where I grew up – a place we both swore we'd never live. I now walk with my child past restaurants I had dates in when I was 16, past pubs I Macarena'd in on A-level results day, past the branch of Boots in which I ate stolen Shapers bars to commiserate over another teenage phantom pregnancy. 'How have I ended up back here?' I think. But I know how. It's for her. For proximity to family and friends, for access to green space and sky. One of my friends said to me recently that having a child urges you to close the loop of your life. And so I've moved my little girl to the place where I was a little girl. I've completed the circle.

She has ruined my life undoubtedly. But unlike in the first year where all I could see was a swinging wrecking ball amid a cloud of devastation, now I view it more as demolishing something in order to rebuild a new unseen future, like an episode of *Grand Designs*. And what is an episode of that show without some mounting jeopardy like 'bespoke hand-crafted 12-foot window doesn't fit', or the less visually impressive, 'crucial delivery of waterproof membrane is delayed in Belgium'. Yet, regardless of what issues the couple building the house face, no matter how many times they've remortgaged or pissed off their neighbours or dealt with a flooded basement, after multiple years and three commercial breaks, there they will be – sitting at a dining table, cradling prop mugs of tea in the sensational home they have battled to turn into a reality. Creating this fresh life has meant sacrificing their old one. It has cost them everything in order to become their *new* everything. You can't have one without destroying the other.

My own post-child 'life rebuild' continues every day. It's still a bit of a construction site. Not all the walls are up, and I definitely still have occasional stints in the on-site caravan but, day by day, I see the progress and beauty of our new hard-fought existence built on the foundations of our old one. It gives me certainty that becoming parents was worth the initial wreckage. Until, of course, our *Grand Designs* episode draws to a close and over a mug of that prop tea, Kevin 'cannot get enough of a gilet' McCloud asks us the ultimate question: 'So, would you do it again?' and at the same time my husband answers, 'No way,' while I say, 'Hmm, not sure,' and then we look at each other and think, 'Crap'.

I thought deciding to have a child in the first place would be the biggest decision I ever had to make. Wrong. The question of the 'second Ratbag' is, for me, a greater quandary. I am increasingly envious of couples who know with joint certainty that they want another one or two or three. They understand what it takes, they know the huge commitment they are signing up for, and yet they are still sure it is the correct course of action, to ruin their life *again* in order to create a new one. I love the idea of another child ripping open gifts under our Christmas tree in ten years' time, but I really can't be arsed prolonging this current period of my life where it takes me three evenings to watch a film because I keep falling asleep on the sofa. And then there is the tricky fact that for a couple divided on the subject of whether to go for another, there is no compromise to be had. Ultimately one of you will get the result you want while the other must swallow down their preference and hope that the residual taste of bitterness fades away. Or perhaps, that the bitterness transforms into something unexpectedly sweet.

I honestly have no idea whether I'll end my life being a mum of one or a mum of two, or a mum of one and a nice dog, or perhaps a mum of one and then surprise twins, or maybe a mum of one and owner of new tits. But what I do know, is that the child I have has been worth all the mess, all the noise and all the destruction.

She has ruined my life in the best way possible.

14

Lessons

As I come towards the end of this book, I realise all the people that I have been in these pages.

I've been a single, negligent aunt. I've been an awful sister. I've been an ambivalent child observer and a bitter, proposal-hungry girlfriend.

I've been a newlywed. A child-free wife reluctantly considering children. A fun-time fertility tracker. A purposeful shagger. I've been a secretly pregnant woman. An openly pregnant woman. A fat-nosed, heavily pregnant woman. I've been a new mum. I've been a lost soul.

I've been a postpartum-poo loo blocker. An Elmo-nursing breastfeeder. A brazen milk expresser. A guilty working parent. A happy working parent. I've been anti-childcare. I've been pro-childcare. I've been a limbo competition winner at an all-inclusive in Majorca.

I've been steeped in a sadness that I am certain will never lift, and I've been happier and more in love than I ever knew possible when it did. I've been a person's home. I still am.

And along the way, I have predictably learnt an awful lot.

Calling parenting 'an education' is like referring to The Blitz as 'quite noisy'. 'An education' suggests neat timetables, method-ical experiments and quiet evening classes in 'Conversational

Spanish'. In terms of 'an education', parenting, on the other hand, has no defined professor, no curriculum, no exam system, and focuses on a subject (child) so selfish and ignorant, it refuses to adhere to the definitions written about it in textbooks.

Parenting is a true sink or swim experience. At times, sinking seems inevitable – you are swallowing so much water, flailing around, not waving but drowning. But you find, over time, that you are, in fact, swimming. Every day. Because there is no other choice. Although, perhaps swimming is too grand a description, for often you are simply treading water rather than completing a record-breaking Channel crossing. *But you're doing it,* and in parenting, you soon realise, that is sometimes the best one can hope for.

Ten things you will learn as a parent:

1) That raisins can de-escalate almost any situation (I imagine I am approaching the time limit on this one, and I quake in fear of that day).

2) How to fold down a pram in the middle of a crowded Sainsbury's car park without resorting to kicking the metal-framed bastard into submission and crying on the shoulder of a kind parking attendant called Martin.

3) That you are actually very talented at Play-Doh and get frustrated when your child wants to 'help' finish your exquisite Renoir-inspired take on Olaf the snowman.

4) That a quick squeeze of a shop-bought baby-weaning peach puree pouch turns any average glass of Prosecco

into a sensational Bellini (I can't remember where I first heard this tip, but I am now lobbying for it to be included in all mothers' first meeting with a Health Visitor).

5) How important it becomes to be able to hide in the kitchen, silently necking Maltesers or trying to suck the crunch out of a Kettle Chip so the child you've palmed off with a satsuma won't discover your treachery.

6) That your child can help keep you fit. Not, as you may imagine by chasing after them all the time, but instead by providing excellent inspiration when you're out for a jog. All you need to do to knock some time off your 5K personal best is pretend that a person ahead of you has snatched your child, and the only way to retrieve them is to sprint up to that person and rescue your beloved baby back. It's dark, I know, but I've tried imagining they've nicked my bag or wallet, and it just doesn't motivate me enough. I'm afraid it has to be 'child' or, at a push, my Nintendo Switch.

7) How appallingly guilty you'll feel when you unwittingly end up injuring your precious little baby angel. Their chubby double chin will get caught in the clip of their bike helmet, and it'll take you far too long to realise why they are crying. They'll get twatted by a swing at the play park when you aren't paying attention and then run towards you for comfort only to painfully collide with your sturdy pubic bone. When it happens the first time, and you're feeling wretched about your poor child, please remember the tale your pal Ellie told you about

a woman who once caught her infant son's tiny ball sack in a zip-up babygro. See, yours doesn't seem so bad any more, does it?

8) That you can really, *really* hate your child. They will wake you up for the hundredth time in an hour and you will find yourself thinking horrible, despicable things. Logically, of course, you know they are just a child being a child, but my god, you have to fight an instinctive physical urge not to chuck them in a bin. Unless you are Jesus Christ himself, you will inevitably, at points, lose your rag. In fact, I would like to see Jesus remain all 'turn thy other cheek' after spending two hours making a lasagne that a small person declares is 'bisgusting' and then chucks on the floor one spoonful at a time while never breaking eye contact.

9) Sometimes your relationship with your child feels toxic. Sometimes it *is* toxic. Every day you are at the mercy of their psychopathic whims. They will earnestly reveal they prefer Wotsits to Mummy. They will steal your dinner and scream if you try to eat anything else. They will refuse to leave the house to go to the park and then when at the park, refuse to leave to go home. They will ask you to read *Zog* and then start howling because you are reading *Zog*. They will make you sing 'Five Little Ducks' but *only* in a Glaswegian accent and *only* the last verse when the mama duck is reunited with her babies because your child lives for drama. You will be gaslit a dozen times before sunset, and each day your spawn will concoct fresh new ways to exert their power over you.

At one stage, my child's preferred method of torment was to order me to take off my glasses and then scream at me to take my hair down. If I refused, she would hurtle over, physically rip the hairband off my head and then lob my glasses across the room because, apparently, she only likes it when I look like the 'after' in a make-over scene from a 90s movie, where a geeky girl's path to happiness involves contact lenses and binning all her Sylvia Plath.

Parenting is a privilege and a joy, but large swathes of it are thankless, unseen, unrewarded and dull. There will be times when you want to escape before you suffocate in drudgery because you can't see how this is possibly sustainable. But then you catch your breath, your child pronounces blueberries as 'booberlies', you laugh, and the clock resets. You're back . . . until the next time they have a shit-fit, and you find yourself sizing up the recycling caddy to see if it could take their whiney bratty mass. And so on and so on and so on . . . repeat until . . . well, until you die, I'm assuming.

I've also realised that 'mother' can be both an act and an identity. Before I had a child, I used to cringe at the amount of parent-proclaiming products I saw – so many businesses thriving on sales of jumpers emblazoned with 'Super Mum' or necklaces declaring the owner a proud 'Mama'. But now I get it. I understand the desire to identify yourself via your dependants. Because to be a mother is to have found your tribe. Yes, a tribe that can be aggressive on Mumsnet about whether children under 18 months should be allowed tomato ketchup (*'Absolutely not! Make your own, free from all those additives, aka POISON. Just simmer some vine tomatoes with Himalayan salt and a teaspoon of manuka for two to three hours while stirring constantly – CHRIST, some women are so LAZY,'*) but still, they are your tribe.

They are other women who understand what it has taken to get where you are and what it continues to take every day. Other women who say to you, 'You got this, mama,' which, while an appalling phrase (because most of the time you feel as if you don't have anything except a huge sleep deficit and suspected head lice), has a kind sentiment at its core. It stems from a place of sisterhood and support. It's one woman saying to another, 'It's hard this, isn't it? Really hard, carrying around all those whirring thoughts, concerns and a never-ending to-do list, but you will endure because it is what we do. I see you. Truly. *I see you.*' A woman buying herself a ring etched with the word 'Mother' is a soldier buying herself the medal no other bugger will award her.

The biggest parenting revelation, though, by a million miles, is that it's true what everyone says about the pleasure children gift you. '*Oh.* So *this* is why people put up with the newborn bit where your life feels haunted. It's because of *this.*' My daughter has brought me a sense of contentment I never previously knew. I was happy before I had a child, but she has enriched what was already there beyond measure – she is a new colour in my rainbow, a new taste on my palette.

It snuck up on me, this love, creeping under my skin as slowly as she once grew beneath it. I love her passionately now. Viscerally. Violently, even. I want to bite her dimpled bum, pinch her chubby thighs, rain down suffocating kisses in an air assault of infatuation.

We read bedtime stories together in the yellow armchair that sits in the corner of her room, as she nestles on my lap. Sometimes we are so entwined I find I have her ear lobe in my mouth that I have been gently gnawing while reading *Room on the Broom*. I crave her closeness.

I want kisses on lips from her peanut butter encrusted mouth.

I want cuddles so tight her arms envelop me like a squid attacking its prey.

I want her spitty little face as close to mine as possible.

I want to glue gun her head to my head and wear her as a noisy fascinator.

I tell my husband these things, and he thinks I'm even weirder than he first suspected. But I don't think it's weird. Intense, sure. Something she may bring up with her therapist one day? Probably. But not weird. It makes perfect sense to me. My girl and I started as one. Instinctively, then, my body is drawn to recreate our original state: a single being with two hearts. We braid ourselves to the other because that is how we first existed.

My love for my daughter is romantic. It is the fodder of movies and fairytales, forever deepening and unyielding. It makes me silly and stupid. It makes me write bad poetry and sickening love letters.

And if I feel this mad, fiery love, I've come to realise, then other parents must do too. The idea of being surrounded by that much unseen pure devotion is almost too much to bear. There I was, living my pre-babe life, not knowing that the whole time, this Earth was bursting and laden with a secret tenderness I couldn't see. Everywhere, invisible exquisite sparkling strands of adoration tethering parent to child, criss-crossing down roads, darting through fields, stretching over cities, over countries, over continents. And I never knew.

And the incredible thing is, that even in the bad and mad times, even when we are certain that our kid is an evil goblin sent from the fiery depths of hell purely to inflict torment upon us, this glittering obsession is still there. Whatever the child has done, whatever the parent may be sidetracked by, wherever the two may be geographically, that connection won't break.

There is a quote by author Elizabeth Stone where she says that having a child '. . . is to decide forever to have your heart go walking around outside your body.' Since I started writing this book, my sister has emigrated to Australia (her husband is Australian like mine – yes, we did probably watch too much *Neighbours* when we were young.) My mum and dad now live in one hemisphere while half their heart lives on a beach on the other side of the world. It's taken having a child myself to truly grasp the depth of the sadness parents separated from their children must live with. But that same insight also provides me with solace, because I know that my parents' love for my sister remains unchanged – it burns as brightly now as she lays on the beach under the brutal Queensland sun as it did when she walked through puddles in grey British drizzle. A parent's bond is the same whether they sleep in the same room as their child, or whether they are separated by oceans. It exists if the child is four months old or 40 years old. It's life's perfect broadband. Fibre optic, super speedy and an unwavering signal in every single room in every single house in the whole wide world. What a gift I had been living with that I have only now begun to truly appreciate.

Occasionally, I get a moment of realisation when I look at my daughter. Like the first time I held her all over again. Another normal day will be happening, she'll be colouring in or dancing to a song she's made up about wombats, and it'll hit me like a wayward branch to the face. *There she is. My girl.* I imagine and hope that as time moves on, these occasional moments of clarity continue. Whether I'm staring at a baby, or a toddler or a seven-year-old reading beautifully, or an 11-year-old trying on their senior school uniform for the first time, or a sullen 15-year-old asking for a sneaky cuddle, or an awkward 18-year-old all dressed up for a party, or a 21-year-old cooking their first roast dinner, or a 30-year-old taking me to an awful bar or a 35-year-old, holding their own newborn, quietly saying, 'Mum. I can't do this. It's just so *hard*.'

There they are. Your child. Built in you and from you. The deepest foundations hewn from those painful, magical early days spent rocking and holding them in the dark. And here you are, sitting in your treasured front-row seat watching them grow up and away, revealing the person that hides within. And then, in my case, you realise your sentimental daydreaming has allowed them to stalk into the bathroom unsupervised because here they are in front of you now, holding a dripping toilet brush shouting 'I FOUNDED A SWORD.'

Sometimes, when my daughter and I are walking along, just the two of us, my girl with her hand in mine, I look down at the top of her silly head as she jabbers on about the time I honked the car horn a week ago that she still finds thrilling, and I know that this is true happiness. This child I wasn't sure I wanted is now everything I could wish for.

I buzz around her, being annoying. Telling her I love her

over and over, hoping the words sink into her bones. She bats me away. 'But will she remember?' I ask myself. Will your kids remember, do you think? Will they know that being an ordinary child born to ordinary parents was the most extraordinary thing that ever happened to you?

To me?

To us?

That, I can't be sure of. But there are some things I do now know with certainty.

I know that you don't have to be maternal to enjoy mothering.

I know that mothering can, in turn, make you maternal.

I know that something can be hard more often than it's easy and still be right.

I know that it's OK to miss your old life desperately and yet not want to trade your new one for all the sapphires and Dairy Milk in the world.

I know that being a mother is my joy, my madness, my exhaustion, my tedium, my bliss, my future and my forever.

I know that my daughter is undoubtedly, my grubbiest, noisiest, most infuriating, most capricious, most magnificent mistake.

Acknowledgements

To all the team at Hodder, especially Myf – thank you for making this happen, and being so patient with my ignorance and enthusiasm – an awful combination you have navigated so gracefully.

To all the brilliant women in my life. My original pack, Girldem – I have no idea what I would do without you. My daily survival crew, The Midnight Commune. My darling Yorklets scattered near and far. The outrageously talented Lady C*nts. My forever urban family, The DPs. My NCT girls who I can always rely on for the perfect welly recommendation. Anna and Sophie for creating pure shonky magic with Marie and Alan. My brilliant agent Sophie. Creative wonder Brona CT, who explicitly told me that a pandemic was not in fact a writer's retreat (sorry for not listening). Felicity W for understanding what it's like to be a clown as well as someone's mum. Ella, my genius pal who thought a perfect gift for a newborn was a bag of exotic fruit. Lyns, the absolute best doctor in town – I remain, as ever, in awe – thank you for always making time for me. And to all the women, both friends and strangers, who sent me messages of support when I was a new mum – those texts, DMs and cards dropped through the letter box meant more than you could possibly know.

Special mentions to LKR – thank you for entrusting me with your story – you're always my person, little one. And to my one true love and professional winner SJY – thank you for always giving me a space to be entirely myself and for making me believe that my experiences may be useful to others.

To my family – forever the best ones.

Mum and Dad – thank you for giving me such a charmed upbringing where silliness reigned supreme. S and I won the parental lottery getting you two. Your unending love and support continues to make everything better. I only hope I can offer the same to your granddaughter.

Shonie – bloody hell, I miss you, you skinny rat. What a wonderful mother those two gorgeous urchins have. Sorry it took me so long to realise how lucky I was to have you near all those years. I can't wait to drink VDCs with you again.

Aus – thank you for giving me half of your beautiful genetic material. I could not be without you, my love. WE couldn't be without you. Thank you for your unfaltering support during the hardest of years. Always my sunflower man.

And to my darling girl who makes my heart soar. Thank you for ruining my life. I wouldn't have it any other way.